Sticky Learning

Harnessing the Power of Educational Software

CAROLYN R. BORTON

ISBN-10: 1501036920
ISBN-13: 978-1501036927

DEDICATION

This book is dedicated to my husband, Jason, for his tireless dedication and support of my crazy ideas and to my son, Benjamin, for being my inspiration to take the leap and follow my dreams.

Foreword

In her quest to make the world a better place, the author invites us to "imagine how amazing our world would be if all people—children and adults—continued to learn and grow throughout their entire lives" (see *F.E.A.R. #3: Summer Breaks Are Good for Kids, Sprint and Recovery*). She advocates Constant And Never-ending Improvement (CANI, coined by Tony Robbins in the 1990's) and Kaizen, from the Japanese words 'Kai' meaning change, and 'Zen' meaning good. Her success is a living testament to continuously striving to learn, grow and improve every day. In this book, she provides you with secrets she has discovered and applied to be successful both personally and professionally.

Although she describes herself as ordinary, she has been able to enjoy a life of extraordinary accomplishments because of her attitudes towards other human beings and the passion with which she pursues whatever she sets her mind to. In this regard, allow her to be a positive role model for you! To achieve phenomenal success, I invite you to take her nuggets of wisdom and apply them in your life.

One of her nuggets is that success lies in constantly increasing our value until we become a key person of influence. As the leader of a successful software development company, the author observes that in the 21st Century, new technologies enable small businesses to compete with large businesses and win because small teams are more agile. Recommending that we focus on quality rather than quantity, she notes that winning in the business arena today is determined by creating value for your clients, and being able to quickly adapt to the changing demands of your market niche.

She acknowledges the significant impact of schooling in her life and those of millions of students in America and around the globe. By going into deep explorations of FEARs (*False Education Appearing Real*) she helps her readers identify much of what is right as well as what is wrong in education today. And, she does not stop there. Instead, she provides a viable solution to the dilemma.

As Carolyn puts it, for schools, "The solution is much closer than we think" (see *F.E.A.R. #6: The Solutions We Seek Are "Over There"*). She proposes that the solution will be found where teachers can be innovative within a framework that supports and equips them to meet the needs of students. Noting that historically no extreme solutions have gotten education out of similar predicaments, she uses the analogy of a swinging pendulum to emphasize the need for moderation, balance and stability in the design of successful school systems.

Her passion for making a difference in education is real and her solutions practical. One solution involves equipping teachers with educational software which customizes feedback and selection of the questions each learner receives for retrieval practice based on the learner's needs. This notion is well-aligned with the current brain and learning research literature.

I agree with the author that to be wildly successful educational software needs to increase student learning or relieve pain that the learner is experiencing. And, I believe that the most successful applications will do both simultaneously.

Like Carolyn Borton, other authors including Malcolm Gladwell (in *Outliers*), Daniel Coyle (in *The Talent Code*) and Daniel Priestley (in *Become a Key Person of Influence*) have recently cited the famous psychologist Erik Erikson whose research revealed that anyone can attain mastery in any field if they simply put in the dedicated time and focused effort. Erikson recommended a minimum of 10,000 hours of consistent, deliberate practice directed towards the attainment of specific knowledge and skills. While this benefit from consistently investing effort to learn might be obvious in areas like chess, it is also applicable to your personal, everyday life. Try it and note the improvements in your knowledge, your competencies, your perceptions of self, and also the perceptions others have of you.

Borton's essential point here is that the only way to become an expert, and be perceived by others as a credible expert is to acquire specific knowledge and skills. And, these are only acquired through consistent practice focused on the attainment of the specific knowledge and skills. Here she confirms Dweck's (1999) point that there is no substitute for hard work.

In her educational software, Borton brilliantly adapts the notion, of getting the job done while simultaneously having fun, that Mark Twain described in Tom Sawyer. She uses games to disguise the monotony and tedium of multiple repetitions while ensuring that the learner remains focused on acquiring the target knowledge and skills. She pays attention to the recall of facts as well as their use in explanations, solving problems, analysis and higher order thinking skills. It is clear that she is familiar with Bloom's Taxonomy and its applications in the areas of assessment, instruction and learning.

To keep learners motivated and informed about their growth and mastery of certain topics, her software enables learners to track their own performance on topics of interest to them. To enable this she provides a bank of parallel formative assessments and empowers students to select assessments which provide them with both retrieval practice and high quality feedback in the areas where they desire practice and feedback. The assessment literature makes it clear that self-regulated learners need all of the above to maximize their learning. To her credit, this math major is applying principles from psychology, physics, IT and business to create educational software solutions.

Importantly, in this book, she provides a roadmap which everyone including software developers, project managers and entrepreneurs can follow to be outrageously successful. For example, in her work, when she observes that weak processes, such as documentation and software, are at the root of a problem, she implements the following process: First, she identifies the problem and gives it a "name." Then, she seeks root cause by continually asking herself: "is this related to 'name'?" If yes, she continues exploring that item. If not, she makes a short note to revisit this question later; as, her experience reveals that, sometimes, after going deeper in other areas, she circles back and discovers that what previously appeared unrelated, is really related after all.

As a concrete example, she described creating a solution for a "time keeping" issue that plagued her for 10 years. She named it "time tracking woes" and gave it three key characteristics: speed, flow and mobility. Speed meant it had to be fast; flow meant it had to fit how she thought her time was flowing from project to project; and, mobility meant she could connect from any place, especially in places where she found herself between meetings. In creating a solution, she paid attention to each path in the process and investigated them to their conclusion.

She also revealed some of her problem solving secrets. For example, when there is a recurring problem and she is invited as a consultant to solve it, she engages in certain specific steps before beginning analysis. She collects data to understand the problem by observing and making notes regarding current processes and procedures, and who is performing them. Then, she applies the following questions:

1. What happens because of this? (What do you observe, what do you want to happen that is not happening?)
2. Who else is affected? (customers, reps, managers, business leaders)
3. What's the cost of doing nothing? (Cost, not just in terms of money, but she also considers the impact on health, stress, time, productivity, and company culture. She often asks: how does that impact your team?)

By following Borton's guidelines, you will be able to successfully identify the most critical problems in your client's current system, and before being sidetracked by anything else, you will be able to focus your solution on the three to five most significant issues. The ability to focus and prioritize, as the author recommends, will bring you much success.

Borton reveals that, in her experience, 9 out of 10 times 80% of surface problems are caused by only two or three underlying root causes. Solutions that deal with the symptoms rather than the root causes are often unduly expensive, and as ineffective as providing a wound dressing when surgery is required to cure the ailment once and for all.

She also provides several practical tips for staying out of trouble during software development, such as "never store passwords in plain text." She remarks that this includes sending passwords between a login page and the authentication function, and emphasizes that "even if you are using HTTPS, encrypt passwords before sending them over the Internet or a mobile data network."

The author also shares keys to success as a designer of software solutions. At the outset, when putting together specifications for a project, she listens attentively to user's perspective and ensures she is able to tell the story of the software from the user's perspective. This technique of listening to gain insight from the user's perspective is the best tool she has found to virtually guarantee that the software she designs and develops "will be useful, usable and, therefore, used."

Borton uses user stories to keep her development teams focused in order to create happy customers and to produce desirable returns on investment. She has found that user stories give clarity to her design teams regarding preferred navigation flow, most used features, screen layout, size of buttons, font size, and how images are incorporated. They, also serve as reference points which allow for "sanity checks" when focus and re-alignment are needed during the design and development process.

Among the other secrets Borton provides are three sets of questions developers can use to determine the best technologies to use for a specific project. She also describes her favorite approach for ensuring she doesn't miss any features when designing software solutions.

In this book, Borton also advises clients who need the services of a software development company, on how to select a service provider. She recommends that clients identify "five or so software companies that are leaders in the right industries for you, then start talking to them about your project. Pass them your specifications. Answer their questions. Then watch for those who want to change the specifications. Ask for explanations why. If they can explain their reasons so that you are able to understand—and believe they are right—then put them at the top of your list." Then, she advises that you create a shortlist and get at least three cost estimates for your project. This process will get you the information you need to make the best decision.

Regarding selecting the right software development company to partner with, she admits that the final decision is part art and part science. It seems intelligent, at this stage, before making a huge commitment and capital investment, that you seek input from an independent, third-party expert who has experience making such decisions. By the end of the book it is clear that Carolyn Borton is a name you will want to add to your network of experts, keep on file, and put in your list of contacts. I invite you to do like I have done: seek her out as an expert, pay for her expertise, and make her a friend!

In the 21st Century to be successful, it is imperative that you be willing to work hard. Dweck (1999) calls this the "effort" mindset. In addition, you need to be committed to meaningful long term goals and be willing to delay gratification as you work toward them. To be my friend you need to be honest, kind and smart. The author, Carolyn Borton, embodies all of these values and much more. She has the full package. So listen attentively as your hear her words of wisdom. Pay attention to the lessons she presents in the upcoming pages and use their message to make your life better.

~ Dennison S. Bhola, Ph.D.
President, Assessment Learning and Technology Solutions

CAROLYN R. BORTON

Table of Contents

CAROLYN R. BORTON

Introduction

Welcome, potential new friend. Though we have not met, I feel I may know you already. Perhaps you might even be a bit like me. Have you had some small successes tucked between mountains of struggles? Do you have several—or many—goals, wishes, hopes and dreams you long to fulfill—including a grand purpose you are still discovering and accepting? Most importantly, do you care deeply that others' lives are made better through your presence and wisdom?

May I suggest you join me on my journey—together—along a path of discoveries, insights, aha moments, stumbling successes and colossal failures? Then maybe I may share with you how I came to know these "magic" keys of learning, what each one means to me, and how I have used and continue to use them in my life. Some lessons have come through people I know, family and friends, or those I met in a fleeting instance. Others found their way to me through people I hope to someday meet. And, yes, more have blossomed from those amazing individuals I will never meet because they passed through this world generations ago.

I would be honored if you would join me on my journey and share your journeys with me along the way.

Blessings on our new beginning...

--- Why Educational Software? ---

> ➢ Because high school students can go from nearly dropping out to applying for college in less than a year.
> ➢ Because a lonely, awkward—dare I say ugly—adolescent girl can experience achievement and gain unprecedented confidence.
> ➢ Because schools have failed so many in my generation and I will not allow that to happen to my son.

The primary driving force in my life is my son, Benjamin. He is eight years old and in third grade. Over the last year I have watched him blossom into a flourishing student. But it wasn't always that way. In fact, when he entered second grade his reading level tested out as 0.9—that's not even fully mastering kindergarten. This was heartbreaking for the overachieving, star students my husband and I were. We were crushed. We thought we had done all the "right things" with private schools and early reading programs. We had given Benjamin so many experiences we'd longed for as kids. So how were we such failures in this area of parenting? The quest for understanding drove me almost to the brink of insanity—at least that's what my husband would say.

I got my first taste of the power of educational software in the early years of the 21st century. At the time, I was working for the third largest educational software company in the United States, PLATO Learning. It was the annual company gathering and a group of high school students was asked to speak about their experience with our software. I was expecting boring, half-hearted and tiresome speeches. Instead what I got brought tears to my eyes. Student after student got up and thanked us for making REMEDIAL reading software. Most of them started our program at 3rd, 4th or 5th grade levels. They were not expected to graduate with their class—

if at all. They were a lost cause. Fortunately an amazing teacher found them, put them in front of the software, and away they went. For most of them it was about a year later and they were applying for college! I realized right then and there that the software I created was powerful and valuable. And I vowed to continue in this field for the rest of my life.

It certainly helps that I'm naturally gifted in this software development. I started designing and coding my own applications when I was 14. I didn't think anything of it at the time. My real wake-up call—quite literally, you will see—came in my final term as a senior in college. I was taking the first real computer class just as a filler before I graduated. I remember being very tired from working on my final thesis for my mathematics major and I fell asleep about halfway through the midterm. I distinctly remember waking up with five minutes left in the class, reviewing my work and handing in my test. My professor knew me from previous classes (as he also taught advanced mathematics courses) so he pulled me aside after class and told me he would allow me to retake the exam. I told him to go ahead and grade it and then we could decide what to do. Not only, did I sleep through half the exam, but I also set the curve for the class. Years later after I branched out as an independent contractor, a book on software architecture found its way into my hands from a co-worker and mentor of mine by the name of Keith. In that book, I discovered that four of the common practices I had developed (with no formal training in software design), used and taught the programmers I led were named as best practices in the industry! It was then I was certain that software was and would also be my passion and gift to share.

This comes full circle back to Benjamin because it was through his adversity that I found the knowledge and confidence to write this book and share it with you. I hope you enjoy it and find some elements to increase your "sticky factor" as you spread your hard-earned wisdom with the world!

--- Why Me? ---

I have often asked myself what makes me qualified to speak about education. Sure, I spent 18 years in school. So what?!? Other people spend more. I've invested twice the amount I spent on my college education on personal development after I graduated from college—and I attended a small liberal arts school, so that's a pretty hefty amount. But again, so what?!? Money isn't everything. Besides other people have spent more.

Honestly, I am not sure there is a short answer. Maybe you will just have to tag along on my journey and find out for yourself.

--- WIIFM ---

When I first entered the field of educational software, all the courseware designers kept discussing this thing called "whiff 'em." Well that's what it sounded like anyways. After several weeks of confusion, I finally had the courage to ask what this was all about and learned it is an acronym: WIIFM meaning "What's In It For Me". One of our unbreakable standards was to tell the students at the beginning of every lesson why what they were about to learn was relevant or useful to them. For example, the multiplying and dividing fractions is important while cooking because recipes often don't match the number of people coming to dinner.

That's a long way of getting to why you might care to read this book.

Perhaps you are a person of influence in your industry - a best-selling author, experienced podcaster, noted speaker/trainer, lawyer or other professional. Then you are likely interested in how to better educate your prospective customers to boost your sales.

Perhaps you are the head of a private or religious school. Then you may be interested in engaging your parents, assessing and tracking student progress, or offering alternative or cutting-edge learning options through educational software.

Perhaps you are a parent interested in better education for your children. Or a software developer looking to bring more benefit to you clients.

Or maybe none of the above. In which case your WIIFM is all your own.

--- My Philosophy ---

My approach to software development has been honed and refined into a simple, powerful process.

Diagram 1: Software Development Cycle

You probably noticed that creation—the building of the actual software—is only one out of the five items. At first, most people are surprised by this. In fact some people dream up a project and expect to pay only for the coding. That is, for only the one fifth of the project that is the "creation". In my experience, this is often THE most fatal mistake of those new to software development.

I invite you to consider the construction of a house. Would you simply arrive on a piece of land with a hammer and saw expecting to start building on day one? And from a sketch on a napkin you made the night before? No...that's totally insane! First, you need to know what you want: big house or small house, one story or multiple stories, number of bedrooms and bathrooms. Second you must have blueprints, permits, and even a piece of land that is properly prepared for your dream home. Third is the critical step of hiring the best contactors you can afford for each element of the construction. Fourth you make a whole host of choices, sometimes compromises for budget or the lay of the land, but certainly colors, styles for molding, appliances, and many other details. At least, after all this, you finally get to get to step five—building your dream home.

In today's world, software generally is not as complicated as a new home. Although there certainly are exceptions. In fact, with nearly every project I have seen, the proper architecture allows you to build multiple smaller "houses" which stand independently or where a small adjustment to a wall will seamlessly join them together later. So you need only build the core rooms you can't live without in the beginning and still end up with a beautiful, flowing mansion over time.

Section I - It Begins with Mindset

In this section, we will explore the misconceptions in education and educational software that lead to frustration, boredom and poor results. In this way, you may remove them from your thinking and avoid them in your own software products.

CAROLYN R. BORTON

F.E.A.R. #1: It's All in Our Heads

"It's all in your head" is one of the most common phases in personal development. That is because it is true.

--- F.E.A.R. = False Education Appearing Real ---

Over a decade ago when I first began reading self-help books, I was introduced to FEAR as False Expectations Appearing Real. This is nice, but my major aha came when I heard FEAR described as "False EDUCATION Appearing Real." In a flash it all made sense. If you think of your life as a prism then you can turn the prism to change what you see. Look at a different side and receive a different "education" on a situation, person, event, or feeling.

As I was growing up, I was constantly (it seemed) pestered by people telling me to "smile more," "lighten up," "laugh." Kids, adults, it didn't matter. Constant and nagging pressure to pretend I was feeling joy when I just wasn't. This lasted from first grade through college and even into adulthood.

You see, my mom passed away when I was very young. Specifically over Memorial Day weekend at the end of my kindergarten year. While I missed her sometimes, I also remember many happy days throughout that summer. Games, play, laughter, and all the rest. It wasn't until I was sent to school in the fall that I was pelted with other people's beliefs that I should be sad, angry, upset. That somehow I was a bad person doing all the wrong things and therefore not honoring my mother and her memory. Very quickly I learned to shut down feelings. I almost never talked about my family, or mentioned I was being raised only by my dad. To the point where I had schoolmates (from the other first grade class) who didn't know my mother had passed away until we were in 5th grade. To atone for a summer of normal kid happiness, I punished myself for well over 20 years. I had lived most of my life in FEAR of all flavors: fear of failure, fear of success, False Expectations Appearing Real and False Education Appearing Real.

I wish I could say it was in the moment of hearing this "education" perspective on FEAR that my world suddenly changed. I knew in that moment without a shadow of a doubt that this was the key for me to unlock my happiness and joy again, but I am still—almost 15 years later—untangling the combination.

Why is this relevant to a book on educational software? Because education is in me. So is software. They are indistinguishable from who I am. They blend into, through and throughout the core of my being.

With any luck—and I hope this is true for you—you have already found your indistinguishables. Possibly you have found them or have not yet been able to identify them as such.

Looking back on my life, it becomes totally clear that "education" and "software" were my quests all along. It took getting out of my own way—realizing certain aspects of my education were "false," identifying them specifically (more on that later!) and having the courage to embrace the education that was the truth for me and release that education that was false.

--- My Obsession with Learning ---

I vividly recall this argument with my cousin...

"Reading," she said. "Video games," he said. "Reading!" she exclaimed. "Video games!" he shouted. "I don't want to play with you anymore!" they screamed together.

It all started when my dad decided that he, my sister (three and a half years younger) and I would take a road trip for the summer. We would take two months and drive from our home in Kentucky down to Texas, out to California, and up to Seattle to reconnect with some of his friends and family and visit really cool places along the way. About a month in, I found myself trapped in Los Angeles at my aunt's house with my cousin. We're practically the same age (he's two weeks older), but just couldn't see eye to eye on anything.

Before school was even out, I begged my dad to get my sister and I some fun games and puzzles to do on the trip. After all, riding in the car for 8, 10 or 12 hours at a time gets really boring. (As you probably guessed this was not our first road trip as a family, so I knew this first hand. And this was in the early-80s, there was no such thing as Nintendo DS or portable DVD players. In fact, CDs weren't even popular yet—if they even existed!) Since my dad was a professor, he of course hooked us up with learning games. I had a whole box of really cool stuff to do. I read every book a dozen times. I would trace mazes from the workbook onto blank pieces of paper so my sister could solve them multiple times.

Let's just say I was crazy in love with learning. My cousin...not so much. All he wanted to do was ride his bike as far from home as possible (sometimes further than was allowed) and play with his friends. After four days of that, I was really missing my quiet time with a good book and working on brainteasers. So we had our argument, spent the afternoon doing our own things and continue—probably to this day—to disagree on what "fun" is.

With education this much a part of me even at eight years old, it maybe isn't so surprising that the concept of "false education" shattered my world. In future chapters, I will share with you some of the most disruptive of these F.E.A.R.s in educational software.

--- The Book that Picked Me ---

"Ouch! That hurt." What just smacked into my toe?

Stuck at the airport. Bored. Tired. Walking around the gift shop just to stay awake so I didn't miss my flight. A book fell—nay, jumped—off the shelf and landed, corner first, on my foot. On the cover is the phrase, "The power of coincidence." Without a second thought, I buy it. There ended my boredom as I couldn't put that book down. I read every word before the plane touched down in Minneapolis.

****

What Book is This?
When GOD Winks: How the Power of Coincidence Guides Your Life by Squire Rushnell

More details available at
www.StickyLearningBook.com/resources

****

In general, I steer clear of religious-sounding books because they make me crazy pushing their agenda of conversion. Fortunately for me, this was not one of those books. Instead as I turned page after page I realized I really should pay more attention to coincidences in my life. And in others' lives. And at my job. And, years later, in my business. In fact, to this day whenever I am working on my business, I will look for patterns and commonalities in our systems or products or purpose and refer to these for guidance.

--- Change Your Hair, Change Your Life ---

I've always had long hair. Well, not always, but since I got jealous of the long hair of a classmate of mine in kindergarten and had a fight with my mother because she always cut it short. Unfortunately, my hair is stick straight. Not one little curl. So about all I can do to keep it interesting is to change where the part falls. I never thought much about that until I used it to change my life.

When I was growing up, I parted my hair straight down the middle. After all, that was the rage in the 70's. Following the poof craze during middle school and early high school (in the mid-80's) I settled on a side part. That is what I took with me to college.

My whole life since I was young, I wanted to be an astronomer. We visited well over a dozen—probably closer to two dozen—astronomy-related sites on the aforementioned trip out west. Even going into college I insisted on majoring in physics as the precursor to graduate school in astrophysics. Little did I know how challenging that would be!

Physics has a reputation in many schools—including mine—as being one of the most taxing majors. Lots of homework, lots of difficult and brain stretching / brain-numbing concepts. Math that would make most people's skin crawl. So as I sat up night after night until one or two am with the others, I didn't really think anything of it. Until electricity and magnetism. I always fancied myself a minor expert on this subject given that I won 1st place trophies in the science fair in back-to-back years, one for a piece I did on lightning (electricity) and another on revealing invisible fields (magnetism). After the first week of the semester, I was a little behind. After the second week, I was overwhelmed and confused. After the third week I realized there was no way I was ever going to catch up and complete the classwork—much less understand what they were so desperately trying to teach me!

So like any "normal" person, I looked in the mirror... and parted my hair on the other side.

Right? Isn't that what you would do first? No? Well, maybe you should try it sometime.

This amazing and bizarre thing happened. I went in a matter of moments from being totally depressed and feeling like I was a failure to feeling on top of the world, excited to release this side of myself that was always pushing and struggling and open the door to whatever was better—and hopefully easier—options that were waiting for me in the future. With complete confidence, I walked into my advisors office and quit my major and his class.

All thanks to the power of my mindset. With my hair parted on the other side, I was now a mathematics major.

--- The Long Hike ---

It takes the harshest of experiences to teach us who we really are inside. As a cross-country runner in my youth, I was well aware of the "runner's high," even though I didn't have that name for it at the time. Athletes speak all the time about "hitting the wall" and how it is what you do AFTER the wall that determines the winners from the losers.

As coaches, mentors, team leaders and parents, we often hear excuses from our followers and children justifying why they want to give up after a small amount of effort. It is one of the biggest challenges to getting someone out of their own way. I often find myself telling my personal story of blasting through my wall. And then challenge others to find their own stories, as nearly all of us have had these experiences, but we typically need some guidance seeing them for what they truly are. Here is my story...

♫ "Just keep walking... Just keep walking..." ♫ In a singsong voice. Spinning in my head. As I slip, slide, and stumble. Mud squishing inside my shoes with every step. Just want to sit down—can't stop— I need to rest! "Please, God, why I can't I take a break!" Another step, and another. "Just keep walking..."

This was the end of what I now call the greatest trek of my life. My husband and I were in Costa Rica. We had just completed a weeklong retreat at a vegan, meditation and massage center. In and of itself that was a life-altering experience.

****

Interested in the Details?
Find out more about this retreat at
www.StickyLearningBook.com/resources

****

Because we were not sure when we'd make it back to Central America, we planned to stay a few extra days to travel to the area around the Arenal Volcano. After arriving, we saw in one of the brochures this hike one could make up to the top of an extinct cone from Arenal which had filled with water. It was advertised to be one of the most beautiful and pristine lakes in the country (maybe even in the America's—I no longer remember the exact wording on the brochure). We asked around the resort and the nearby visitor center about how long the hike would be. The standard answer was 45 minutes to an hour, round trip. They said it was a slightly challenging hike, but totally doable for a couple in their early 30's.

So away we went. Enjoying this beautiful hike, first along the dirt path through grassy fields then up the side of this hill covered in tropical rain forest. The higher we climbed, the steeper and steeper the path became. Near the peak, we were pulling ourselves up using branches and roots of the trees. We came down on the inside of the crater and indeed the lake was as beautiful as advertised. Serene and peaceful. We rested our tired feet by wading into the quite, chilly lake. Ok, cold would be a more accurate description. We were already pretty tired, as the trek up was well over an hour. But we figured the way down would be a bit easier because it would be downhill and we had already walked the path since we were returning the same way we'd come.

What we didn't account for in our youthful arrogance was rain. After scrambling up the inside and climbing backwards down the outside of the cone for about a half hour, I was completely exhausted. Done. Finito. I could have rested for a while right there on the path, but it wasn't meant to be. As we got to the part where walking (in a sliding fashion) was possible again, it started raining. Fortunately it was a warm tropical rain, but the dirt path quickly turned to mud. And it was still quite steep. So now instead of walking we were sliding on almost every step.

Without missing a beat, my husband breaks out the tune from *Finding Nemo*. We convert it to "Just keep walking" moments later. As we continue, we pick each other up after each slip/fall. Somehow, someway, what seemed like hours later, we made it to the bottom. We trekked back across the prairie, past farm buildings and to the visitors' center.

We looked awful. Mud head to toe, inside every layer of clothing. We bought flip-flops at the gift center so we could walk back to the hotel. Just to make sure we didn't miss anything, we also walked over the rope bridge, around the bend in the river to get the premier view of the waterfall, which crested outside the visitor's center. The stares from other visitors was enough to tell us they seemed to think we were homeless bums who crawled out of the woods after months of being separated from society.

Just to be certain we would always remember this experience, we memorized the sign for the lake on the mountain: Laguna Cerro Chato.

Back at the hotel the shower looked like a muddy stream. We were so tired, we decided to go to bed early, well before dark. And then... it happened. We heard thunder outside our room. Then it repeated twice more and my husband looked out the window. Instantly he called, "Come now! You've got to see this!" I thought he was crazy for showing me a stupid thunderstorm. But he was right.

It was no storm...the volcano Arenal was erupting! Fortunately, it is kind of like Hawaiian volcanos where a bit of rock and smoke go into the air (that was the "thunder" we heard) but mostly beautiful red lava flows down the side. Instantly we were wide-awake. We sat for over two hours at the restaurant in the hotel, eating dinner and dessert and watching this amazing spectacle. Remember, that was after we could barely crawl into bed from a day of extreme hiking.

Isn't it a wonder what we can do when think we can't do any more?

I challenge you to look back at the toughest, most miserable, most painful moments of your life and find your own "Laguna Cerro Chato."

****

Share Your Story
www.StickyLearningBook.com/contact

****

F.E.A.R. #2: High Grades = Quality Education

It's just so ingrained in our western culture: Better grades mean you are smarter than someone with lower grades. "A" students are the best. "B" students are the second best. And so on. These are facts. No one would argue them, right. And if they do, that's just crazy talk!

Or is it...

To make our kids feel better about themselves we say things like "Grades don't matter. We'll love you anyways." While there is truth in that, there are nearly no parents that will buy a kid an ice cream sundae with all the fixings to celebrate a D on a report card. But what the heck does a D mean anyway? It means you tried really hard not to learn. An "A" means you tried really hard to learn, and learned some stuff, just long enough to pass a test on it. What kind of learning is that anyways?!?!?

--- Okay to Forget ---

The sad reality is that common practice in learning is training to forget. We attend seminars, take a ton of notes, start implementing new ideas and practices and quickly go back to our old habits. Somewhere in grade school we realize we only need to remember what we learn long enough to pass a test on the material.

In Freshman English class, I remember the teacher telling us how we would prepare for finals. We had studied close to 100 short stories, poems, and non-fictional texts throughout the year. Most we hadn't even thought about in months, so being a class of over-achievers, we were very nervous. The teacher, however, proposed a creative solution to our dilemma—we would each review our notes and do a short presentation on the key points we would need to know for the final exam. The catch was that we would not find out which text we would speak on until we arrived in class on our assigned day.

I was very excited for my turn. I had reviewed and re-reviewed my notes. I felt prepared. Until... I drew my assignment and it was "The Grapes of Wrath." Wait...that's a novel. Yes, apparently the teacher assumed we all understood we also needed to review all our notes on the novels as well. Which I had not done. If you look in the dictionary under "train wreck," you will find a reference to my talk. I couldn't remember anything of significance. I remembered there was a drought. I remembered they worked as laborers on farms. I remembered they got trapped on one place because they couldn't buy their way out. That was it. Pathetic. And I knew it. To add insult to injury, the teacher proceeded to "help" by pointing out the many things I missed. Including the myriad of religious references, which I will continue to remember are there, although not the details of what they were exactly, for the rest of my life.

The point is that because of the emotional impact and the fact that I knew this would make a great story someday, I chose to remember many details of the experience. However, the parts I deemed were not important are now forgotten. This is the same for nearly everyone—I'll give exception for the truly unusual people born with photographic memory. Although a friend of mine from 6th grade who had this gift, told me she controlled it by saying "snap" when looking at a page she wanted to remember. Her experience was that the time it took to reread a full page of text in her mind made her too slow when taking tests. So often she learned identical to the rest of us, and then locked in only certain pieces as photographs. Best of both worlds. Yet still prone to forgetting when that was allowed, accepted or expected.

--- Cramming ---

One of the consequences of training ourselves to forget is cramming to make up for it. We stuff our minds full of facts at the last moment so we can recall them from short term memory. As if somehow our brains have limited storage capacity.

****

Research Shows...
Storage is not lost, it is the connections that dwindle and degrade when not used. Read more at
www.StickyLearningBook.com/resources

****

Back in college, at the end of winter term my sophomore year I put my cramming skills to their ultimate test. I had fallen behind on term papers for my class on the history of India. My mathematics class required both a final exam and a major project in *Mathematica*. My physics class had a take-home exam and lab reports with extensive data analysis in Excel. I had a hard deadline when my roommate and a friend of ours were leaving on a trip to California for Spring Break. I was not going to be left behind! Couple that with an intense fear of failure (meaning bad grades caused by incomplete work). I managed to squeeze all that work into seven days and sleep a total of seven hours in the process. Not seven hours a night, seven hours total. That's the power of motivation, grit, adrenaline and the body of a 19-year-old. Honestly, I don't remember most of the trip because I was asleep in the back seat. My first real memory from the drive is waking up at dawn as we came over the mountains and saw Las Vegas in the distance.

--- The Pressure of Straight A's ---

For many years, I was totally caught up in the lie that A-students are better than others. Specifically because I was a "straight-A" student. Other than one extreme exception (handwriting), I carried straight A's from second grade through 8th grade.

Well almost.

I was devastated and crushed by a B in English in 8th grade. Even more so what hurt was that I received an A first quarter and a B second quarter and then a B overall for the first semester. To rub salt in this wound, several of my friends (each male, although there's no way to prove that was relevant) received split grades on the quarters, but an A overall for the semester.

I was convinced this teacher had it out for me because I told her earlier in the year that I would like more to do because the class "wasn't stimulating enough." In reality there's a really good chance I used the word "boring", which I am sure didn't help my case.

The sad truth is that I can't remember anything we learned in that class. (I'm sure you would be hard pressed to recall 8th grade reading and writing facts if I put you on the spot right now.) In reality, this grade didn't matter AT ALL for going to college, or everything else I believe was ruined at the time. I am willing to bet none of my clients check my 8th grade report card before hiring me. Not even my high school or college grades.

Yes, a Ph.D. is a great thing. It is proof positive of perseverance and hard work. And those with doctorates get a little more clout than those of us that decided we couldn't wait any longer to start making a difference in this world. But all it really means to me as an employer is that someone has the fortitude and grit to stick with a program until it is complete and that they know how to dive deep into one subject. This is important, and yet...

There are many real-life stories of high school dropouts that went on to become extremely wealthy. So much so that there was a time in my life that I wished I had been a dismal failure in school so I could use that to drive me to financial success. (Did you catch that this is another instance of F.E.A.R.?) We will get to the bottom of this misconception in a future chapter.

--- Standardized Testing ---

One more factor that cannot be ignored which pressures us to make short-term decisions about our education is standardized testing. Teachers are under intense pressure to meet minimum standards. Not only do they have to show adequate growth for the year, they also have to overcome the lost learning from the summer break. The only way this is feasible is to teach to the tests. Unfortunately, this reinforces the students to forget what is not on the test, even when that knowledge would benefit them more in real life. However, the saddest part for me is that those straight A students are the ones most crippled by these trends.

They get good grades. They do well on standardized tests. They graduate top of their class. They get into a good university or college and also succeed there. Finally they graduate ready to rise to the top and be successful quickly as they have done their whole lives.

For some this happens, but for many it does not. Instead reality hits them and hits them hard.

Success as an employee is little like success in school. So they jump out of the rat race and become an entrepreneur. Probably because of a great book they read (for me it was *Rich Dad, Poor Dad* by Robert Kiyosaki) or a motivational seminar (or 10!) they attended.

Now they are even worse off. To succeed with your own businesses takes even more skills that school does not prepare us for and which certainly are not on any standardized test!

Or maybe it's not them; maybe it's just me...

I do not intend to imply that standardized testing is the cause of the rash of small business failures every year. Rather I see this as proof that standardized testing is in no way shape or form an indicator of success in life.

F.E.A.R. #3: Summer Breaks Are Good for Kids

Swimming and playing outside, residence camps, day-after-day spending time with my friends. These defined my summers as a youth. Inevitably these ended when school started again in the fall and then all we could talk about was how much we had forgotten.

--- Outliers ---

The first time my eyes were opened to the true determent of summer breaks on kids was while reading the book *Outliers*, by Malcolm Gladwell. In the book he discusses the statistics of how summer breaks hurt poor kids more than wealthy kids because the wealthy kids actually continue their education through the summer, even though it is not formal schooling. Average test scores start out statistically equivalent in kindergarten and by 5th grade they are undeniably different.

I personally only noticed a partial decline in myself because even though my family would have been classified as lower-middle to middle class, both my parents graduated from college (where they met, in fact), my father earned a doctorate (PhD) in physics and was a college professor. My mother's father was a top PhD research scientist for Standard Oil. In other words, school mattered a lot in my family—but not just school, learning. That was the key. Learning was built into practically everything we did as kids. Anytime we improved a skill, in anything that mattered—school, sports, music— we were rewarded with a special dinner, dessert, book, toy or other surprise. On every family trip, we would plan to visit museums, zoos, state or national parks or tour a facility of interest to us.

However, my friends didn't have the same experience. It wasn't that school wasn't important in their families. It was just approached differently.

I remember very clearly making one of the biggest faux pas of my life, in part, because of this. Actually, it lead to my first fist fight. In the fashion of inexperienced kids, I said something really stupid to my best friend's sister. Specifically, her sister was one year behind us in school. And I told her that I thought my friend would end up in her class because her grades were not as good as mine. I thought I was being sneaky and said it in a whisper and all that. I didn't count on my friend's sister telling her the details. A couple days later, my friend found out and got so mad that she threw icy snowballs at me—which is a real challenge in Kentucky, come to think of it—and she jumped me from behind and punched me in the eye with one of them. I freaked and ran home (kiddy-corner across the street) without even defending myself. This has been a source of embarrassment for me for most of my life. After studying learning practices and building educational software for almost 15 years, I now realize there were so many more factors than just stupid childhood arrogance.

--- Attachment ---

So why are we so attached to "the old ways?" Precisely because they are old, meaning established. In addition, the damages caused by the breaks is only seen over an extended time frame. It is the compounding of the effect that is devastating.

****

Read More on Compounding
One of my favorite books on small actions affecting
big results is The Compound Effect by Darren Hardy.

Check out this book and other great resources at
www.StickyLearningBook.com/resources.

****

We have wonderful memories from our summers off and believe we will be cheating out children of those same memories if we take the long summers away. However, I challenge you to find even one example where your memory spans the entirety of 10 weeks. Even though you may have many good memories from one summer, each is probably less than a day. Certainly less than a week.

--- Sprint and Recovery ---

So then what's the alternative to long summer breaks?

The most successful athletes rely on a training routine called "sprint and recovery." The concept is that you push yourself—hard. Ideally past the point you believe is possible—called "the wall." Then, they rest. Purposefully. With as much focus and "effort" as the training sprint.

Scientific research and the success of sites like *Lumosity*, clearly indicate that the human brain also responds well to this form of training. In fact, a few colleges have even adopted the idea. For example, Cornell College in Mount Vernon, Iowa is known for a One-Course-At-Time program where students take only one course in a three and a half week term with a long weekend to ten days off between terms. Various countries in Europe and Asia, send their children to school year-round with about a month off for summer and winter breaks. Clearly this approach has some benefit as these countries score higher than the US on standardized tests year after year.

****

Going Deeper
For more information on Cornell College
and to discover my personal connection, to go
www.StickyLearningBook.com/resources

****

So the solution is quite simple: keep our kids in the learning process. In fact, this shouldn't be limited to kids. Just imagine how amazing our world would be if all people—children and adults—continued to learn and grow throughout their entire lives. We could be nicer, more compassionate and understanding, bringing more value to those around us both professionally and personally. So the key then is not just a technique—like Sprint and Recovery—but a mindset of Constant And Never-ending Improvement. The Japanese have used this method, CANI or Kaizen, for years. 'Kai' meaning change and 'Zen' meaning good.

F.E.A.R. #4: Success in School Determines Success in Life

Culturally, we are programmed to believe that those who are successful in school will be the most successful in life. But is that fact or F.E.A.R. (False Education Appearing Real)?

****

One Example
Steve Jobs dropped out of college and later
founded and grew the Apple Corporation.

For more articles and books on this topic, go to
www.StickyLearningBook.com/resources

****

While there is a correlation between success in education and success in life, there is not causation.

In fact, there are other factors that determine success in life besides simply success in school. Of course, that does not mean school isn't important. Quite the opposite. Being successful in school, in fact, is evidence you have already mastered SOME of the skills needed for success in life, such as determination, perseverance, and basic time management, to name a few.

On the other hand, failure in school can drive a person to excel DESPITE this setback. One example is Russ Whitney, a high school dropout, who became one of America's youngest self-made millionaires at the age of 27.

Personally, I received my bachelor's degree in Mathematics with Magna Cum Laude status (in other words, high grades, practically straight A's). But if you had seen me back at the end of third grade you would have said I should pursue anything but math. It was not a good subject for me. I almost failed multiplication tables. Week after week we tested. We had to pass each number in order: 1's, 2's, and 3's and so on up to 12's. I got completely stuck on 6. I worked every night practicing. I used flash cards, I took practice tests. No matter what I did when test day would come, I just wasn't fast enough to finish or I had so many wrong answers I didn't pass. I was devastated. After a month, I finally passed 6's. But then 7's and 8's were just as bad. I was SO frustrated because I knew I could pass 9's, 10's, 11's and 12's, but I was not allowed to try. As the weeks remaining in the school year whittled away, I was sure I was going to have the first non-A on my report card in years. Given that I lived for the praise I received from my good grades—I was known as the "star student"—I was especially crushed. It was only because my father stepped in and pressured the teacher to let me test 9's through 12's in the last week of school that I was able to save my A after all. Nonetheless, that winter and spring of constant struggle stuck with me throughout the rest of my school years, including after I declared my major to be mathematics. I received that degree for perseverance, not for my innate ability to comprehend complex mathematical concepts or solve difficult problems.

****

Thank you, Russ

Although he may never see it, I would like to give a shout out to Russ, the head of the Math and Computer Science tutoring center, for supporting me in getting my degree. It was his endless patience and clear explanations and assistance that got me through all those classes.

****

--- What Matters Most ---

So, if success in school is not the determining factor for success in life, then what is? There are many schools of thought (pun intended) on this. Brian Tracy, professional development trainer, suggests it is self-discipline. Darren Hardy, editor of *Success Magazine*, says it is focus. The great spiritual master, Jesus, says it is love.

Personally, I believe these can all be summed up into one overarching principle: Constant and Never-ending Improvement. In other words, if one continuously improves oneself, then successes or failures in the past and present will not be a reflection of successes in the future.

In fact, failures may be reframed as opportunities for learning. Resilient people use the lessons from failure to become greater or more successful than they were before the setback. Even the published, peer-reviewed psychology literature suggests that life is all about learning.

CAROLYN R. BORTON

****

First Source
For more details on the sources that influenced
my understanding of success, please go to
www.StickyLearningBook.com/resources

****

--- From 4th to Last ---

Just in case you don't believe me yet, let me tell you a story from my own life...

In high school, I ran with the "smart kids." There were five of us who shared the spotlight for all the academic awards year after year after year. I graduated 4th in my class (out of 89). I was accepted as early admission to one of the top 10 liberal arts colleges in the U.S. I graduated Magna Cum Laude. By all external measure of schooling, I was a top performer.

My husband was even more successful. He was so smart he was ostracized by the "smart kids." He graduated fourth in his high school class of 400 and would have been Valedictorian if he had taken study hall instead of band his senior year. He took every chemistry class offered by our college, not just because it was his major. In addition, just for fun, he also took the most difficult of the physics classes and most of the junior and senior level math classes as well. He also graduated Magna Cum Laude.

Fast-forward three years. At this time, we were married and we decided to open a business together for our hobby, ballroom dancing. By this time, we had won medals at more than a dozen

32

competitions both regional (Midwest) and national. We were regularly training at the same studio as four of the six top amateur couples in the country and we were their friends, even though we were 10-15 years younger.

We were at the height of success and climbing higher. We were in the right place at the right time. We even had a lot of the right ideas.

So then why four years later were we shutting down the business, donating most of our inventory (which we couldn't even sell at 90% off) and sitting on a mound of debt? Because despite all of our success in schooling, we had no training in business and entrepreneurship. We read and studied extensively during the experience, but it amounted to too little, too late. After running the numbers what seemed like 100 different ways, we took the best and most viable option available.

With our tails tucked between our legs, we both got "regular" jobs. In fact, I had never left mine, but it was around this time that I shifted into the industry that would soon become my passion.

Little did I know what rainbow was waiting after this storm.

CAROLYN R. BORTON

F.E.A.R. #5: If It Worked Before, It Will Keep Working

Have you ever heard the expression "If it ain't broke, don't fix it?" This appears to be wise on the surface, but have you ever paused to consider if this might be just another urban myth?

Consider a car—brand new, driving off the lot. Smells great, drives great. What would happen if you waited for there to be a problem to take it in for its first maintenance check? By then you would likely have driven tens of thousands of miles. Most of the time on old, worn out oil. And the tires would likely be worn thin as well. This car would not only be a hazard on the road, it would also be expensive to repair. Instead, what is the best approach—regular maintenance and tune-ups? In other words, we are all fixing our cars BEFORE they are broken.

Similar analogies can be drawn on nearly all electrical and mechanical equipment. Lawn movers become unusable and unrepairable in about four years, if they never receive maintenance. On the other hand, regular tune-ups and blade sharpening will allow a mover to last for many years, even decades.

Technology is evolving at a rapid pace. And the rate of change is increasing as well. Unfortunately education and training are lagging behind. In fact they are being out distanced by technology faster than they are evolving. In other words, the gap is expanding exponentially.

--- From Industrial Revolution to Information Revolution ---

In the Agrarian (farming) Age, "school" was learning a trade from a skilled master. Bakers trained bakers, farmers trained farmers, and blacksmiths trained blacksmiths, and so on. Reading and writing were luxuries and not necessarily needed to be super successful in one's craft. Once trained, a person tended to stay in their career for their whole lives. By continuing to improve their skills, a person could become sought after and by providing exceptional value, earn exceptional income.

With the Industrial Revolution came the shift to assembly lines. Workers became as interchangeable as the parts the factories produced. The training to operate a particular spot in the "machine" was minimal. Being exceptional at the skills of one's career at best earned a cost-of-living increase each year. There was now a big gap between the value of managers and the value of workers. And the hurdle to being a factory owner, and therefore the wealthy elite, was insurmountable for the average person born into average means. Meaning the children of factory workers became factory workers. Formal schooling established in this age was created specifically to produce the best possible factory workers.

Fast forward to the Information Age. If you look closely, big businesses are still very much as they were in the Industrial Age. Now their product is information. Still the schools most valuable product is more factory workers and ones that are better at producing information.

However, new technologies change the playing field completely. Small businesses (4/8/12 people) are able to go toe-to-toe with large businesses (hundreds of people). More and more we are seeing small businesses win because they are more agile and able to adapt to the whims of the market place. By the time they are gobbled up by the large businesses, the wave is waning and those same entrepreneurs can turn around and build another small manpower, big dollar volume business. No longer is business dominated by quantity; it is now dominated by value.

So what does this mean for the schools? They are producing a crop of students who will enter the workforce and be un-valuable. Even those with high level degrees from highly respected colleges and universities will be little better off than those who graduate high school. Because the skills they are learning and mastering are not valuable skills to entrepreneurial businesses. A new approach is needed, and fast, if we are to save today's school children from this horrific fate.

--- Changing Forces ---

Even in my own business, I have talked myself out of paying attention to warning signs. In November of 2010, we invoiced our best month ever. In the first week of December I diligently prepared work orders and made sure my teams were firing on all cylinders. For I was going to be out of town the entire second week of December on vacation in Cancun, Mexico. And, for the first time since starting my business in 2002, I was planning to not check emails or call into the office for the entire nine days of my vacation. My staff was left with strict instructions to text me if anything came up that required my attention.

Alas, the vacation was miserable. Cancun experienced the coldest weather on record for at least the last 50 years. The resort was centered on swimming—their claim to fame were the swim out rooms. But it was just too cold. At most we would find a dozen people around the pool in the peak of the afternoon. We have pictures of me watching a sunrise wrapped up in the heaviest clothes I brought, plus the resort bath robe AND a couple towels from the room. It was Cancun, after all, so I never thought to pack winter clothes! Little did I know this was a foreshadowing of what I was to find when I returned home.

Two days into my trip—on Monday of that week, to be exact—one of the clients realized they had an error in their accounting department and put all our projects with them on hold. That was half the team put on the beach all at once. And that was only the start of the pain. Also in December, my biggest client switched from sending us checks to auto-payment to our bank account. Every year they make their January payment on December 31. In past years, it came by check. I didn't realize they were switching to account transfer so soon (since they said that would start in 2011). So we drew zero expenses against that payment. And it was our largest ever. It meant we received 13 payments in the year (when in the past we properly only received 12) so the tax burden on it was harsh. Between our business taxes and the flow-through to our personal taxes (because we were an S-corp at the time), we got killed. So much came out in taxes, in fact, that I LOST money on our biggest invoiced month ever.

Needless to say, I was crushed. We had worked hard. More than that, I had worked harder than ever before (which is saying a lot because I've always had the reputation as a hard worker, often the hardest worker among my colleagues). After this blow, I lost my way. I felt like I was sitting on the sidelines just watching my company shrink and shrivel all around me. I lost my will to get up early and stay up late. I lost my ability to keep my promises to save my clients at the last moment when they forgot to prepare for deadlines. In short, my world fell apart.

To add insult to injury, the technology scene shifted. Practically overnight. One day we are building Flex applications, as we'd done for over five years. Within the course of one month, all but one client was talking exclusively about HTML5 applications. Several even cancelled their approved Flex projects to pull back and switch to HTML5. Of course they saw us as "their Flex guys" so most went out for bids from other developers. When we had been their exclusive team for years and were known to be reliable.

Overall I equate it to being kicked while you are down. Repeatedly. And knocked down again every time you get up. Until you start to believe you may not have the strength to get up again.

Fortunately for me it was in 2011 that I discovered martial arts. But not just any martial arts, one specific school with an unusual philosophy for the industry.

--- KMMA ---

Krav Maga Martial Arts, in Lutz, Florida, is run by 6th degree Blackbelt, Shihan Stephen Del Castillo. What makes his school so different is that it centers on positive praise, confidence building and the life skills of martial arts. Their modality is based on the best self-defense system ever created (in my opinion), Krav Maga. Which doesn't mean much, unless you are a bitter, kicked down, entrepreneur and mother of a very energetic boy of five, who fell in love with martial arts at three years old and insisted on going every week, twice a week for years.

The magic happened when they offered a special program for families to purchase a lifetime membership. With my son so gung-ho for so long (two and a half years at this point), I knew instantly it was the right move for us. Right at that same time, my son graduated into the older class—which was for kids, teens and adults. The next thing I knew, my son was dragging me out on the mat to participate. The last thing on my mind was working out again (I was a desk-chair potato) and while I was a chronic worrier, I didn't believe I could ever learn to defend myself.

I couldn't have been more wrong. I fell in love with martial arts, initially with the forms and katas, then later with the self-defense. As with anything I am passionate about, I went in 110%. I worked extra hard to catch up to my son and had the honor of testing for Blackbelt with him back in September of 2013. Words cannot describe the excitement, honor and pride of that day. Not just for my son, but for myself. KMMA—and specifically my Blackbelt test— gave me back my self-esteem, confidence and never-quit attitude. Before the test, I totally dismissed Shihan's talks about how those three hours would change your life. I thought, "That's for the kids, it doesn't really apply to adults." Yet again, I was proven wrong.

So what's the lesson?

1) Synchronicity happens in mysterious ways.
2) Change is inevitable: expect it, pay attention to it, and keep flowing with it.

As my husband likes to say about his white water canoeing experiences: To maintain control and get through safely you must travel faster or slower than the rapids. If you let the environment carry you, you will end up on the rocks every time.

F.E.A.R. #6: The Solutions We Seek Are "Over There"

The pendulum swings back and forth; often at maximum extremes. In the school system, it shows up as

- Large classes, small classes
- One teacher, multiple teachers
- Emphasis on enrichments, focus on the core subjects
- Freedom for teachers to design their curriculums, classwork developed by experts outside the classroom

For professionals, it is a bit more subtle and complex. Start a career or new venture and it is new and exciting. Every day is full of learning and first-time experiences. Let's call this "newbie heaven" where happiness and motivation are high. After a while, you start to get into the rhythm. This turns into a march or a marathon that seems to go on without end. Same old stuff day after day. Let's call this "droning worker bee." Once we finally get fed up enough, what do we do? We look for the "new hot money making system" and we jump on board. Again the excitement and happiness jumps up and we're in newbie heaven again! Sounds good, right?

We'll all accept the fact that every time we jump into newbie heaven, we reset our earning potential. We're back to having a ton of fun, but earning peanuts. Barely paying our bills—if we're lucky enough to even do that! More often, we are shelling out money—sometimes at alarming rates—to learn faster and make "the big bucks" we were promised.

Yes, of course, there are people who are wildly successful in our new favorite industry. But these are neither the newbies nor the worker bees. Instead, they are the people that stuck with it, put in the extra hard work, and continued to grow their skills and increase their value until they are the most influential people in that industry. Everyone looks to them for advice. They set the trends. The best projects are offered to them first, and the rest of the crowd is fighting over their scraps.

--- What's the Solution? ---

Stay put, go deeper, build value, get famous—at least with those people who matter, the people within your industry and who rely on your industry.

The most insidious example, however, and the one which kills more businesses than anyone would care to admit is the pendulum on entrepreneurs. Imagine three circles drawn so they overlap just a bit in the middle. Label them "solutions," "money" and "joy." Nearly all entrepreneurs have two out of the three. For example, do-gooders have amazing solutions and lots of joy, but more often than not they're broke. Stock brokers have solutions and money, but little joy—they do what they do for the money. Scam artists have money and joy, but often no solutions—and you can probably think of a half dozen people or businesses masquerading as viable companies who are actually scam artists when one peers beneath the veil of their solutions. Inevitable they will a get return on this "investment," sometimes in very public ways. (Did you think of Enron just now? I did.)

Well, for most good, honest, hardworking entrepreneurs, they realize there is an imbalance—that they are missing a piece to the puzzle of success. So they go chasing it. Unfortunately, in the process they leave the other two elements behind. In order to pursue joy, the stockbroker quits and moves to an ashram (a religious retreat) in India to meditate with the monks.

The reality is that with any pendulum, the most stable and successful point lies in the center. The sweet spot for entrepreneurs is the intersection between solution, money and joy.

****

Entrepreneurial Sweet Spot
For more details, check out *Becoming a Key Person of Influence* by Daniel Priestley and other information at www.StickyLearningBook.com/resources

****

The success for professionals lies in pushing through the worker bee though constantly increasing their value until they emerge in the center and rise as a person of influence. For schools, it is the middle ground of allowing teachers to be innovative within a supporting structure, and meeting the needs of students with the right mix of individual and group instruction with small and large classes and enough enrichments mixed with core subjects.

No extreme will do. And the solution is much closer than we think.

CAROLYN R. BORTON

Section II - Software as a SOLUTION

You may be familiar with SaaS as "Software as a Service." In the modern world of software, as of this writing in 2014, this is almost always a given. Of course, software is a service. It is everywhere—our computers, our cell phones and other mobile devices. It is even in our cars as satellite radio, GPS and safety features that automatically call for help even if you are unable to! Even the largest sellers of installed software—Adobe, Microsoft and Apple—have transitioned to subscription services in place of boxes on shelves.

Therefore I choose to use "SaaS" to mean "Software As A Solution." Meaning that software has the potential—if designed and built correctly—to solve many of our F.E.A.R.s.

CAROLYN R. BORTON

SaaS #1: Adapt to the User

The goal of educational software is to impart knowledge, be helpful in a moment of need, or provide a momentary or lasting benefit. At the end of the day, for educational software to survive, it must fill a need—solve a pain—which the learner is experiencing. Adapting to the user means engaging the learners where they are, with the skills they have and engaging their interests to keep them progressing. Some clients, with their own excellent staff, delve into this themselves, while others outsource it to companies like ours.

This does NOT mean cheesy settings on panels for colors and backgrounds. That is so 2004. Rather, this means track every move a user makes and use this to improve their experience. In some cases, trends seen across many users give the best picture to drive new phases of development—enhancements, new features, better flow and User Interface (UI). In other cases, the behaviors of individual users is more significant. For example, Google Maps has mastered the individual user experience for searches by showing your most commonly searched and most recently searched addresses as soon as you click in the search box to type. I estimate that 40-50% of the time, the address I want to use is already there before I enter a single character.

Video games are the ultimate adopters of this methodology. Let's take, for example, the Mass Effect series for Xbox and Xbox 360. Depending on your decisions as the player, the members of your team change their dynamics with each other and perform differently in the mission sequences, including who survives in the end.

In educational software, the most significant uses of adaptation are

> - **Pre-assessments** that allow learners to test-out of skills they already have, and focus their studies on skills they need to learn or improve.
> - **Learning-on-the-edge** which means learners are presented with questions, tasks and assignments that are right on the edge of their current skillset meaning they feel confident they can succeed and are still learning and increasing their skills along the way.
> - **Auto-tracking** progress which means the learners, teachers, instructors, parents or supervisors may be able to see a chart of their increase in skills any time they want.
> - **Subjects-of-interest** keep learners coming back because they are excited about the materials and increase the learning because learners feel a personal connection to the content, especially when cultural overtones or personal experiences are incorporated.

Unlike conventional teaching, educational software puts these elements within easy reach and even allows them to be combined!

Not all educational software needs to be complicated, spanning multiple ability or grade levels and covering many subjects. Instead, it is often the most simple—and therefore focused—training programs that have the greatest impact.

SaaS #2: Build Confidence

Back in 2011, my son convinced me to try my first martial arts class. At the time, I was 36 and had been doing little besides working behind a desk for almost a decade. I was super skeptical that I would even make it through one class. However since I had been watching him for a couple of years, I figured maybe I could fake my way through. After just a halr hour, I was tired, but feeling very good about myself. I wouldn't find out the secret for over a year.

I started training to help as an assistant instructor at the dojo. Part of this training was, not surprisingly, the philosophies behind the successful training program. This school had one of (and probably THE) highest Blackbelt ratio in the area and the highest ratio of ranked Blackbelts. Another thing I didn't know when I started is that "Blackbelt" is just the beginning of the levels of mastery and only means you know the techniques of the system when asked. The degrees of Blackbelt: Shodan (1st degree), Nidan (2nd degree), Sandan (3rd degree) and so on, indicate true mastery of more and deeper skills in real world situations.

The biggest contributing factor is a key characteristic I did notice when my son first started: positive reinforcement. But more specifically, their philosophy is that when training beginners, the focus should be 70% on building confidence and 30% on technique. In other words, you can't let them hurt themselves, but it is more important for them to feel good about their punches and kicks than getting every technical detail correct. The negative or harsh critique should be strictly avoided. Now, as students level up these ratios change so at an intermediate level it is even 50% confidence and 50% technique, then advanced level the students are already able to separate critique from their self-worth so the ratio flips to 70% technique with a continuation of confidence building at 30%. Finally, once a student passes their Blackbelt test—which I can say from experience is the ultimate test of endurance and mental toughness—their confidence is so strong they can now focus 90% on technique as they prepare for the higher and higher ranks.

As I considered this philosophy, I realized it was a great model for employment as well. What if an employee, especially youth, could start out in a new position with training in this fashion? As they "level up" they would take their confidence with them so employers and bosses can focus a higher percentage of their time on technique. Then step back further and imagine this was the way of the school systems. It might just blow your mind—as it did mine—to consider the awesome effects this would have on society in the future.

--- Skill Dependent ---

Many self-development experts in the 20th century were promoting the idea that building self-confidence would universally translate to all areas of your life. While there is a small truth to this, as shown by it working for a small percentage of the population, I believe that the actual truth is far more complex. Although it can be captured by a simple concept: The degree to which confidence will increase in an area of one's life because of success in another area of life is directly proportional to the degree in which the skills for success overlap. For example, confidence because of success in math classes will increase confidence significantly in physics class because these subjects have significant overlap (that is because Newtonian physics is the application of algebra, calculus and geometry). However, high confidence in a technical skill such as computer programming or accounting, has almost no impact on confidence with relationships, either personal or professional. This is exemplified through the terms "geek" and "nerd."

An interesting possibility with educational software is the blending of skills in ways that allow users to feel successful a significant portion of the time. It is human nature to continue to do those things we like—those things we feel we are good at. As an example, let's imagine a learner has the ability to absorb science concepts easily, but they struggle sometimes with history. If they could be introduced to the history of science, from the science angle, then they will start to "get it" and feel better and better about their skills eventually resulting in the ability to study and learn general (non-science) history more easily. I know this to be true as this example is my own experience.

The effects of skill dependence on confidence is another example of how subjects-of-interest is a key to educational software.

--- Disguised Repetition ---

In 1993, the famous psychologist Anders Ericsson debunked the myth of genius—the myth being that one is born a genius or not. Rather, he explains, anyone can be a master or even genius in any field if they simply put in the effort. In short, this can be thought of as 10,000 hours of **focused, directed practice with proper guidance and coaching**.

While it is true that every person need not be a genius in every subject, there is a certain amount of practice required to get "good enough." In the martial arts, they say, "Your side kick doesn't approach 'good' until you've thrown 1000 sidekicks." But if beginners were forced to throw 1000 sidekicks before moving on to more complicated kicks, many would certainly quit before getting to "the fun stuff." And they would certainly never achieve mastery or a Blackbelt. The same can be said for many subjects in school and even with important skills needed for success in a career, with relationships, or any worthwhile endeavor.

The secret to getting the practice is to disguise the repetition. This means games, fun activities, friendly competition, rewards or achievements. It also means a misdirection of focus to a "fun" aspect while incorporating the less-fun activities over and over. A new term has sprung up for this in the software world—gamification. It simply means to add the aspects we all love about games—goals, prizes, competition and collaboration—into an "ordinary" piece of software. One example I heard about recently was a mobile application for sales people to track their prospecting goals. There were tons of built-in rewards and badges for everything imaginable—from the obvious ones like beating goals and being the first to make 10 cold-calls in a day to less obvious ones like being the first to get three clear no's in follow-up meetings or having the guts to tell a bad prospect they weren't a good fit before the prospect said it.

Disguised repetition can also be achieved with what is known as a "circular" or "spiraling" curriculum. This is a somewhat common practice in grade schools, but not as common in adult education. Somehow we seem to think that this switch goes off when we enter the workforce that says humans suddenly learn differently. In reality, we are all still children inside and especially when it comes to study and learning we tend to fall back on our engrained patterns and habits. The most successful education—both in and out of software—will introduce a concept at a surface level, then move to other concepts (also at the surface level), looping back over and over again each time adding new and deeper aspects. I often describe this in general terms as three levels: technique, principle, and attitude.

Take any skill—say typing. The first level of skill is hitting the keys to make words. Then one can add deeper skills, such as typing with multiple fingers. The principles behind this include speed, effectiveness of communication and an underlying attitude of constant and never ending improvement which leads to communicating more information, more effectively, and more efficiently to establish oneself as a valuable asset to others.

CAROLYN R. BORTON

SaaS #3: Track and Reward the Right Things

So if there are the "right things" to track, you may be asking yourself, "What are the wrong things to track?" and "Why might someone be tempted to track them?" First let's consider the "why", then the "what" will become most obvious.

In fact, the "why" can be summed up in two words: fast and easy.

Let's do a thought experiment... Imagine you are tasked with sharing one of your skills with a large group of people (at least 30). Now imagine each day when you meet you will need to provide a report on how much they have learned and who the top performers are. In fact, the pay you receive for the day before is directly based on these measurements. Well, that means you have about five minutes to make a determination of how much money you will take home each day based on your success—or lack of success—on the day before.

What would you do?

a) Teach something that is easy to convey, like facts and formulas or processes.
b) Teach something that is easy to measure, like knowledge recall.
c) Track the amount of work each student is doing to determine how good they are at the work because you don't have time to look at individual or complex results.

d) Rank the students into simple categories. Perhaps something like: lost, confused, okay, better, and best.

Does this remind you of a system you experienced before? Maybe for 12 to 16 or more years of your life?

Granted as you moved up in grade level, especially post-secondary, the work may have been at deeper cognitive levels involving analysis and synthesis. And you may even have had the fortune, at one time or another, to be given scores based on mastery of the various topics within a course rather than strictly a summary grade. However, nearly all of us experienced some equivalent of the A-F or 4-point grading system. And we are putting our kids through the same system as well. We even continue to use this system with employee trainings and evaluations.

Unfortunately, this means we are tracking the wrong things. We are tracking how much work learners are doing over how much learning is taking place. We are tracking the first attempts students make at solving new-to-them problems, thereby, training them to be scared to try new things lest it "hurts their grade." We are encouraging cramming over long-term skill development, and seeking shortcuts over repeated, focused effort.

So what should we be tracking?

--- The Right Thing #1: Cognitive Level ---

Clearly recalling facts, memorizing specific texts, and identifying trends are important skills. They are the foundation of higher levels of cognitive understanding. And they are ONLY the foundation of higher levels of understanding.

Diagram 2: Representation of Bloom's Taxonomy

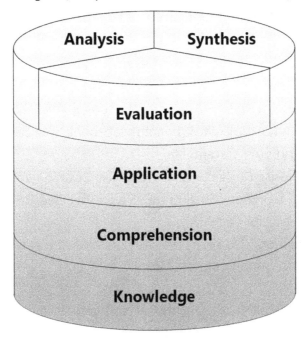

There are a variety of different ways of categorizing levels of learning. Bloom's Taxonomy is my favorite reference model for understanding how learning increases with practice and guidance.

The foundation is *knowledge* upon which *comprehension* is built. This is the stage where student's move from recalling fact to interpreting meaning and extrapolating connections. When this is stable, learners are ready to *apply* this knowledge and solve new problems in different ways. The highest level is shared equally by *analysis* (the breaking apart of information), *synthesis* (the joining together of information) and *evaluation* (forming opinions and judgments).

Asking the right kinds of questions is critical to evaluating a learner's cognitive level. For example:

- Knowledge: What are the benefits of regular exercise?
- Comprehension: Compare the benefits of cardio vs. weight lifting?
- Application: Which form of exercise is best for a body builder and why?
- Analysis: List five exercises for toning the legs and which ones have the highest benefits for runners. Include details to support your statements.
- Synthesis: Design a 3-day exercise rotation for an overall body workout. Explain how you decided to group the exercises for each day.
  Evaluation: Do you feel that marathon runners should practice running sprints? Why or why not?

One of the benefits of educational software is that a computer never gets tired of asking questions. It can be told how to ask the same question 5 different ways. It can ask the questions before the learners have studied the material deeply and offer insightful feedback to keeping learning at any and all of the cognitive levels.

****

Formative Assessment
This is also known as Formative Assessment. For more information go to www.StickyLearningBook.com/resources

****

In fact, computers can also monitor a learner's answers and ask questions based on how well they are doing. Thereby avoiding frustrating the students by asking too many questions beyond their level as a paper test might. Especially when you consider that many learners are often in the same classroom at the same time and each has their own understanding and mastery of the material.

****

How to Write Questions
If you would like more information on how to write good questions for each of the cognitive levels, check out the free resources at http://www.StickyLearningBook.com/resources.

****

--- The Right Thing #2: Summative Assessment ---

There are two primary modes to assessment—the measurement of learning:

> Formative: while the learning is "forming"
> Summative: the "sum" or amount of learning that has taken place over a period of time

Formative assessment is where learners are assessed in how well they understand concepts, which may be new to them or new details and/or depth within the concepts. These assessments may be given within a few days, hours or minutes after the learning occurs. It is most effective when integrated DURING the learning process, especially when the results are used to guide further learning.

The brain-enhancement site "Lumosity" has several games which utilize adaptive learning. Every time you get a level correct, you progress to the next higher level. If you make a mistake, you get another one at the same level. If you make a mistake again, it moves down a level. By using this approach they keep the users right at the edge of their comfort zone, which is the best place to increase skills. Also, this gives the user small wins about half the time so they feel encouraged and hopeful about trying again and again. Finally, this gives the most accurate measurement of current skill level. (This is technically a "summative" characteristic, and is why high-stakes tests like the GMAT for graduate student applicants also use this technique).

The scores for formative assessments are useful to instructors or teachers as a way to identify in what areas they need to improve their communication of the material because students aren't "getting" it. However, formative assessments should NOT be used as a measure of the students themselves. It can be easy to stumble into this trap accidentally by including the "number right" from homework or classwork practice questions in overall grades for a course. Instead there is a better measure for this practice which we will discuss later (see the section titled The Right Thing #3: Rewarding Effort).

Summative assessment is exactly what it sounds like—a measure of skills at the moment the test is taken. By giving equivalent summative tests over time, the increase in learning can be tracked, plotted and rewarded. These would be better 'grades' than the traditional ones. And some schools have even adopted them, although they are far from wide-spread.

****

Summative Assessment
Read more at www.StickyLearningBook.com/resources

****

Adult education tends to include more of the right things than public schools, colleges and universities. Although there is still a strong tendency to include formative assessment scores in overall grades throughout education.

--- Case Study: Parachute Packing School ---

Let's look at example to illustrate how mixing formative and summative assessment scores may be misleading.

Take a look at these three students and their scores on the end-of-week exams.

Diagram 3: Packing the Parachute

WEEK	STUDENT A	STUDENT B	STUDENT C
1	60	80	90
2	75	75	95
3	85	85	90
4	100	90	100
5	100	100	90
6	100	90	100

Who do you want to pack your chute? Student A, right?

Let's look closer at some common numbers used for overall grades.

Last

> ➢ Student A = 100 = A+ = Certified
> ➢ Student B = 90 = A/B = Possibly Certified
> ➢ Student C = 100 = A+ = Certified

Average

> ➢ Student A = 87 = B
> ➢ Student B = 89 = B
> ➢ Student C = 94 = A

Weighted Average (last half matters more than the first half)

> ➢ Student A = 91 = A/B
> ➢ Student B = 89 = B
> ➢ Student C = 95 = A

Hmm, those didn't tell us Student A is the best option the way our guts did. Maybe some other statistic will?

Median (middle)

> ➢ Student A = 93 = A/B
> ➢ Student B = 88 = B
> ➢ Student C = 93 = A/B

Mode (most)

> ➢ Student A = 100 = A+ = Certified
> ➢ Student B = 90 = A/B
> ➢ Student C = 100 = A+ = Certified

No, that's not working any better. While the statistics might certify Student A based on "last" or "mode", it would just as likely pick Student C who intuitively we would probably not want to be our parachute packer.

So what's REALLY going on here? Student A started off slower on the learning. The instructor must have noticed and changed tactics resulting in significant increases in understanding. Student A finally mastered the techniques in week four with repeatable results through week six. So it would be most appropriate to categorize the tests in weeks one through three as *formative* and weeks four through six as *summative* for this student.

Now if we run new scores only for the summative period in the last 3 weeks, we'll find:

- ➤ Student A = 100 = A+
- ➤ Student B = 93 = A/B
- ➤ Student C = 97 = A

Now it is clear that Student B and Student C need more training since they are still not CONSISTENTLY meeting the strict standards (of 100% accuracy) after six weeks. As well as Student A clearly passing the certification.

--- Assessments in the Real World ---

You may be wondering at this point if it is realistic for all learners to achieve 100% scores all the time. While this is a wonderful dream, the answer is clearly no. The level any learner needs to reach in any subject is determined by the consistency of the results required.

For parachute school, nothing less than 100% for three (or arguably more) weeks is acceptable, and followed up with regular retesting and recertification.

In most learning situations 70%, 80% or 90% over some appropriate period of time is "good enough." So if this were, say, culinary school and these students were learning to be master cake bakers, they could probably all be certified with these scores. This assumes, of course, that critical skills like food safety are worth more than 20% of the summative assessment so they can't completely bomb one critical factor and still be certified.

However, what is most important from the example of the parachute school is to recognize that creating grading systems that include scores from the learning process will produce undesirable side effects. First, the learners with the highest mastery of the subject matter may not be the ones with the highest score. Second, grading students' guesses while they are learning makes high-achievers scared to try new subjects. Because there is no way anyone can score 100% on day one at a new endeavor. This means the system is training the potentially best and brightest to stay in their comfort zone and end up mediocre.

Fortunately, there is a simple solution. And it comes in two parts:

- Only include in final grades the tests that summarize the students' learning (summative assessments)
- During the learning phase, reward the effort as much or more than the correctness

--- Right Thing #3: Rewarding Effort ---

What you focus on expands. By focusing on effort, you will get more effort. More effort = more focused practice = gradual improvement over time. This is simply how the universe works.

The myths of "he was born talented" and "she is so smart" have been debunked by psychologists and those who study the nature of success. In fact, those we consider geniuses simply have put in 10,000 hours of concentrated practice on the subject of their passion. Child prodigies included.

I read about this concept several times before I had the pleasure of seeing it in action. Specifically while training to be a martial arts instructor.

Our motto is "be a good-finder." That hyphen is very important. It means find the good in what the students are doing, even on their first day when they are likely doing much more incorrectly than correctly. If you look carefully enough you can find SOMETHING to praise. Even if it is only the effort!

When I am assisting in class, I love to find those little things to praise. The pride that kids feel when you find something they are doing right when they feel somewhat lost and confused. In fact, it is even more powerful for adults, especially when they grew up in a critical household or currently have a critical boss, spouse, friend or all of these!

By feeling good about doing something right, learners will be more open to receiving help and corrections. Then by being rewarded both for the effort to make the correction and achieving the correct result, their effort will "double down". This continues and upward spiral of success.

Success begets success. Success begins with effort. So let's reward the effort, and the success will naturally follow.

SaaS #4: Make Learning Feel Good

In my experience, the natural follow-up to the effort-success spiral is feeling good about oneself. Having confidence one's abilities makes us, as humans, more likely to try new experiences. Those at the top are able to give the most back to society, thereby making the world better for everyone at all levels.

We've already discussed several ways that educational software can make learners feel good. Now, let's review them all in one place.

--- Adapt to the Learner ---

Present learners with materials at and slightly above their level. Always. This keeps their motivation and the feelings of success high, which in turns makes learners want to continue and perform the practice they need to achieve their desired level of mastery.

Whenever possible, present materials that are culturally relevant and of interest to the students. Some students love astronomy, others prefer historical novels. In many situations, such as reading and comprehension practice, the subject matter can be flexible. Make it so!

--- Unlimited Practice ---

By rewarding effort, educational software is able to keep students practicing almost indefinitely. My son put at least 100 hours into his math practice using his iPad because every 5 questions right gave him a virtual fish to put in his virtual aquarium. And there was no punishment for getting a question wrong, he simply moved on to the next question (a variation of the question he missed). Whether right or wrong, the feedback reinforced the correct answer. Brilliant!

In fact, today's children regularly put hundreds of hours of practice into video games. As a result, they can see and process small changes in visual data and respond to them with their fingers before they can even say what they see out loud. What is commonly criticized by my generation (Gen X), may in fact be a valuable skill in the future work force. Even better would be to use educational software to build upon this skill and create a generation of super-fast readers.

****

What's in the Future?
In fact, I am working on a project along these lines.
Keep tabs on our progress by following my blog at
www.StickyLearningBook.com/blog

****

--- Available When Needed ---

My son is a morning person. I am not a morning person. It is a significant blessing to me personally that he is able to not only be entertained, but do valuable learning and practice in the morning before my neurons are able to make sensible connections.

Also, there is a major benefit to learners to have a question and be able to solve problems in the moment they are experiencing them.

Feeling angry? There's educational software for that. Need to know how to long division? There is educational software for that as well.

****

There's Educational Software for That!
For specifics, go to www.StickyLearningBook.com/resources

****

Decades ago, computer-based trainings were delivered through mainframes and required users to go to special labs to access them. Internet-based trainings shook up the status quo and have offered learners the opportunity to study both at home and at school. The upwelling of home schooling is proof positive that this works.

Now we are facing a new age where mobile devices are in the hands of learners every moment they are awake. Also it is not uncommon for learners to access multiple devices each day. There are new and emerging technologies on the horizon. Someday we'll be developing for glasses or implants or whatever else science fiction—and science reality—can dream up.

--- Never Get Tired ---

Computers can ask 10 questions or 100 and never complain or get bored or wish they had something new to look forward to. Computers don't judge—even accidentally—whether a learning is taking "too long" to progress to the next level. Computer won't compare one learner to another thereby making one of them feel superior and the other inferior.

69

Assuming, of course, they are designed properly. After all, computers are really only as good as the instructions put into them by us. This is why the proper techniques and systems are important in designing and building educational software. This is why this book has an entire section dedicated to this topic. Turn the page to get started.

Section III - Harness the Power

In this section, I will reveal my personal process for creating exceptional software. Not just "good", not event "great." Nothing less than "exceptional" will do.

****

My Personal Motto
Exceptional Software, Revolutionizing Education

****

The following processes are powerful. They are the keys to my over two decades of success developing applications. They have survived the ebb and flow of platforms: Windows and Mac to Web to Mobile. The surge and resurgence of languages: FORTRAN, Pascal, C, C++, Perl, PHP, ColdFusion, ASP, ASP.NET, C.NET, HTML/JavaScript/CSS (a.k.a. DHTML), ActionScript, HTML/JavaScript/CSS again (HTML5), AIR/iOS/Java, and more.

From 30,000 feet, there are five main steps to take: prepare, specify, evaluate, decide and create. Each one embodies a wealth of knowledge—quite possibly a full book on each. The following chapters will give you the key components of each step and equip you and your team to create "exceptional software."

CAROLYN R. BORTON

Power 1: Prepare

Before embarking on any trip, we begin with proper preparation. The better the preparation, the better the experience. Software is no different from a family vacation in this regard.

The most effective, most efficient and sanest way to prepare is by tackling each of the core components for preparation separately.

- ➢ Identify and quantify the need
- ➢ Determine why now is the right time
- ➢ Observe what you are doing now
- ➢ Avoid unnecessary risk

--- Good to Best ---

Good software fulfills a need. Great software fulfills the need better than any non-software process could. A simplistic example is that a calculator is clearly superior to pencil and paper for long division. The best software fulfills the need better than any other available software.

One example for me is software for tracking time. For over a decade, my consulting business was paid for the time we put in (and occasionally for materials we purchased, such as stock photography). Tracking our time was non-negotiable. Yet, every day, every week, every month I would have to track down developers who had not completed their time entry. One of the worte offenders was, in fact, me. Every program we tried was difficult to use. They loaded or refreshed too slowly. They didn't record entries in a way that matched how I worked. Specifically, as the leader I am touching many projects throughout the course of a day as each team reports status, requires input of some kind and even as I specify and design the next piece of educational software that we are going to build. I remember my day as one flowing timeline from project to project. Most time keeping systems track entries at the daily level. For years, even those that allow you to start and stop a "clock" were strict about using it in-the-moment and really challenged you if you had to go back and make entries or changes. I found workarounds, but they were never perfect. The closest I could get to "perfect" was recording everything I did in Outlook as meetings. This worked for the most part, but still was awkward and slow, especially on days where I was pulled in many directions. I had to be very careful that my calendar didn't end up showing on screen-sharing unless I wanted to hear gasps from the other participants!

This was the norm until six months ago when I found a relatively new player in this market—Toggl. (Yes, it is spelled correctly with no ending 'e'). Frankly I got lucky because they were in transition between versions so I was able to work in both for a while. The new version totally mastered the art of on-the-fly tasks. With fast auto-complete, continuing tasks later, simple configuration for my team and many other features I loved. In addition, the old version totally had back-data-entry down pat. I would completely use the keyboard (no mouse required) because it remembered date selections and had obvious tab-order. Wow! I am in heaven now as I use this. In fact, over the last six months I have only seriously fallen behind once, and that was with only five days missing. I considered this to be a small time window as I was previously often 10+ days behind or with 10 out of 14 days missing or incomplete.

Long story short, the right software solved my problems. So now I am a raving fan (in case you weren't sure) and I promote them to all my friends in the consulting industry. Even if you don't bill clients by the hour, just tracking where you are spending your time is extremely valuable. It can expose weaknesses that you don't even know you have. For me it was watching training videos or playing with other peoples educational software. I love online education so much I can easily get side tracked into exploring someone's site or video stream and lose hours of my day. By tracking this as a separate task in Toggl, I am acutely aware of when this "addiction" is being productive—as I need to spend some time to keep up with trends and happenings in the business—and when it is taking me off task and distracting me from my key goals.

In my experience, this is often the easiest step to take. As a business owner, I know there are bottlenecks and kinks in my business. Aspects where we just don't meet our full potential. Sometimes it's friction-filled team dynamics; sometimes it's a mismatch between the people and the roles (and occasionally just the wrong person). Most often, however, I find that it is the processes—including documentation and software—that are at the root of the problem. These weak processes are causing the other symptoms. It is at this time that I sit down with the process I am sharing with you in this section and use it to better my own business.

So how do I set my goal? I take a very high level look at the problem and give it a "name." In this way, as I am taking the next steps, I can ask myself "is this related to 'name'?" If so, I continue exploring that item. If not, I make a short note to revisit this question later as sometimes after going deeper in other areas I will circle back and discover it is related after all.

Here's an example. Go back to that time keeping issue I told you plagued me for 10 years. I named it "time tracking woes" and gave it three key characteristics: speed, flow and mobility. Speed meant it had to be fast to make entries or there was no way I would use it— ideally making/switching entries as the phone was ringing for my next conference call. Flow meant it had to fit how I think about my time as flowing from project to project. Mobility meant I could connect from any place I happened to be working and especially when waiting in other places between meetings as this was my prime opportunity to stay on top of it and not fall behind.

Here is a worksheet I use for myself.

Diagram 4: Table of Specification Worksheet

Overview of the Problem:

Name It:

Key Objectives:

1.   2.   3.

Be More Specific (for each Key Objective):

1.

2.

3.

--- Determine Why Now Is the Right Time ---

Once you have your goal laid out all you need to do is ask yourself, is this a big enough problem at this time to dedicate a week of my life to it? In other words, stopping all other work, going on hiatus or sabbatical and putting a full 40-60 hours into solving this problem. If the answer is no, then I offer for you to reconsider tackling a custom software project at this time. If the answer is yes, then why is it that important? This will be your answer to why—or if—it is time to solve this problem now.

While sabbatical is the most effective way to get the clarity and focus to solve problems, it is not always practical in the business as it is running right now. So the process I am teaching you is designed to work, even if you must spread the effort out over several weeks.

--- Study What You Are Doing Now ---

In order to truly know what your software needs to do, you must first study and understand what you are doing now. Some steps might currently involve software. And some might not. It is very important to include BOTH in your notes.

While working with a mobile pet grooming company, I spent a couple afternoons with different groomers. I learned more about the weaknesses of their current software from what the groomers did NOT do as from what they complained about. What I mean is that they were quite hesitant to ask to set up the next appointment because their current software was hard to use on their cell phones. They were required to log in every time and navigate through multiple screens to even be able to see the schedule and offer appointment times to the customer. Then it was highly likely they would, without realizing it, be forcing themselves to drive across town between appointments because in the booking software the customers' addresses were buried about three clicks away from the calendar schedule.

This was not just a problem for the groomers, but it caused headaches for the booking agents, the managers and hurt the bottom line of the business because they were literally walking away from sales. The owner knew that driving across town was a problem—that was why he called for my help in the first place, but without the thorough observation, he probably still wouldn't understand why the re-bookings by the groomers was such a problem. No amount of training would get around the pain of using that system the way it was. Fortunately a simple, targeted, mobile application—built specifically for the groomers—was a simple and cost-effective solution. And it even allowed the owner to guide and enforce best-practices when the groomers were out in the field every day.

--- Check the Paths ---

Next, pay attention to each path your process can follow when there are options. For example, a customer might see a television ad and then call or go to the company's website. While the end result might be the same—placing an order—there will be important differences in parts of the process that you need to take note of so you may ensure all the aspects flow smoothly once your new software is in place.

I use several different approaches to capture the notes on what is being done now.

1) **Freeform**: brainstorming—just capture it all in the order you observe it
2) **Organized**: checklists and flow charts—get clear on each step
3) **Screenshots**: highlight problem places
4) **Ask the team**: their personal prioritized lists

Most often I use a mix of these. In an ideal world the timeline and budget would allow for a thorough working through each of these. In reality, I go with what my gut says is the best for each encounter until I start seeing trends forming.

--- Go Deeper ---

Now that you have notes on what your current processes and procedures are and who is performing them, it is time to start some analysis. The goal is to lead yourself to the top three to five problems in your current system so you can properly focus your solution. Through years of going through this process, I have found there are only three questions that truly need to be answered.

➢ What happens because of this?
➢ Who else is affected?
➢ What's the cost of doing nothing?

It really is this simple! Don't let the simplicity fool you into adding complexity just for the sake of complexity.

Let's take a deeper look at each of these questions.

****

Imagine the Universe...
Imagine the universe. Galaxies, stars, planets, life. It is governed by simple rules such as gravity (F = Gm_1m_2/r^2) and conservation of energy (E = mc^2). Why should the design of software (of any kind, educational or otherwise) be any different? In fact, it is the simplicity that makes this such a powerful technique.

****

--- What Happens Because of This? ---

By starting with "What happens because of this?" it tends to get our brains outside of the box of just semi-blindly repeating tasks just because "we've always done it that way." Instead, you are seeking a deeper truth. Think of this as a funnel. You are sliding down the sides from high-level rational thinking to the emotional impact, and eventually to the PERSONAL impact. If not answered directly, then follow up with the question, "And this is a problem because..."

Repeat this question at least three times. By diving deeper and deeper, you will get to the real problem behind the problem so that it can be addressed. In my experience doing this analysis with my clients, I have found 9 out of 10 times that 80% of the surface problems are caused by only two or three underlying problems. If we just solved the surface issues, they would spend many thousands of dollars on bandages that would never truly address the surgery that will cure these ailments once and for all.

--- Who Else Is Affected? ---

Sometimes this is obvious, sometimes it is not. I encourage my clients to dig into this even if there's not much impact from the previous question. On more than one occasion I have found this will lead to valuable—and money-making or cost-saving—insights. For example, I was working with an agency who needed their sales reps to report when they arrived at a client site and when they left. Whether they checked in or not didn't seem to matter to the reps at all. After digging deeper, we found that the software made it challenging for them to check in quickly, so whenever they were running too close to their appointment time, they would just skip this step. Well the result was that the managers would end up calling them—often in the middle of an appointment—to check in and find out if they arrived. This interrupted the flow of the appointment and possibly cost the company sales (at least it would if they had visited my office). It was only by looking at others affected—in this case the managers—that we were able in fact to find the ripple effect of this skipped step, and trace it back to the people doing the skipping.

Just to clarify this further, when interviewed, the sales reps complained that one of their frustrations was that their managers would call multiple times every day to check in on them. So the owner of the company was pressuring the managers to be nicer, but then every time he would ask for progress reports, the managers had no choice but to call. In the end, it turned out the limiting factor was that the sales reps would get logged out of the system during appointments and while they were driving due to inactivity. Because their username and password wasn't remembered, they had to type it in every time they wanted to connect. Then they had to click through multiple screens to get to the check-in and check-out buttons. In other words, it ended up being less painful to get called—and later complain about it—than it was to follow the best practices.

The solution was to create a mini-application the sales reps could install on their cell phones which remembered their username and password for the system and presented them with quick check-in and check-out buttons right on the main screen. This removed any excuse for not taking the 10 seconds to check in or out and repaired at least that part of the relationship between the sales reps and the managers as well as the managers and the business owner.

--- What's The Cost of Doing Nothing? ---

The key with this question is to focus not just on money. Also consider the effects on health, stress, time, productivity, and even company culture. Often I will ask this question in different ways, depending on the flow of the conversation. Some examples include, "What is that costing you?" and "How does that impact the team?"

--- Putting it into Practice ---

So what does this analysis look like when you do it for yourself?

> Step 1: Print out (or photocopy) one of your processes.
> Step 2: Go through it line by line and answer these three questions.
> Step 3: Realize that many lines may have answers like "the work gets done," "none," "nothing," "this is an easy thing to do" and "it is being done by the right role in the company." If so, this process is relatively healthy, in fact.
> Step 4: Repeat for the rest of the processes you have documented.

> ➤ Step 5: Review the results.

The "art" of software design steps in at this point. First, you will notice that a half dozen to a dozen or more steps jump out at you as having a significant impact on the company. This might be dollars, or it might be stress, or maybe there is another "cost" such as time or productivity or number of people affected. A few of these steps will already be "under control", which means that you have minimized any losses significantly already, so while they have a cost, there is not much more that can be done with them.

--- Case Study ---

Here is a real-life example of this question and answer process that I went through with a client who sent service reps out to people's homes and was frustrated with their current booking and customer management system.

Step: Make three clicks to view the customer's address. (Click their name to see their general information then click the "more link, and finally click the "details" tab and scroll down.)

Q: What happens because of this?

A: Because each click requires a webpage to load, it takes between 15 and 20 seconds to view a customer's address.

Q: And this is a problem because...

A: We need the address in order to know if the new appointment we are trying to book is nearby. Because we usually have to go through multiple existing appointments to find one that is close enough, we are making the person booking an appointment wait one to three minutes before we have a suggestion for them.

Q: What happens because of this?

A: Customers get frustrated, especially new customers. (Recurring ones have accepted that this is just how it is.)

Q: And this is a problem because...

A: 10-15% of new customers never book an appointment because they get frustrated with waiting and give up after one or two suggestions that don't work for them. About half of our customers only ever get one appointment or only call when they have a discount coupon.

Q: What happens because of this?

A: We are not making the sales we need to make for the amount of advertising we are doing. We're reaching new customers and getting them to call, but then we lose the sale before it happens.

Q: And this is a problem because...

A: We are on the edge of profitability right now. We need each advertising effort to yield better results for the bottom line.

Q: Who else is affected?

A: The appointment reps are sitting around between appointments or driving across town, which really stresses them out, especially if it is during rush hour.

Q: What have you tried to do to solve this problem?

A: We tag each customer with their zip code so we can see that on the main screen (without clicking their name).

Q: And how well did that work?

A: It reduced the number of customers we need to click on and reduced the give-up rate by about 5% (it used to be closer to 20%). We have received few complaints from reps about driving long distances, but it will happens two to three times per week per rep so I hear about it at our monthly team meetings. We have seen no noticeable improvement in the second appointment rate.

Q: And how much is that costing you, monetarily?

A: Well, we're probably losing two to three potential new customers per day, plus three to five re-bookings for follow-up appointments. Per customer, a sale is on average $100. So all told, that's five to eight lost opportunities per day, or $500 to $800. Times 22 working days...Definitely over $10,000 per month and possibly over $15,000 in some months.

Q: How much is it costing in time, stress or other factors?

A: The whole team is sick and tired of this issue. Managers are tired of hearing the reps complain about driving all over. Reps are tired of not having enough work, since part of their pay is commission. I am tired of losing potential profits month after month after month. In short, this is an underlying stress in the company that is affecting our culture and how much we enjoy our jobs. Everyone on the team loves what we do, but HOW we're doing it has got to change.

As you can see, the benefits of asking these kinds of questions illuminates deeper issues and underlying factors which can now be addressed by the software. This will produce a much better solution than if only the surface issues are resolved.

--- Avoid Unnecessary Risk ---

The final step in preparation is to understand the data you need. Specifically getting totally clear on what you absolutely must have and what would be nice to have. The more data you store on a person, the more likely it is that are you encroaching on PII— Personal Identity Information. In plain English, this means you have enough bits of information on a person to know exactly how they are and even possibly steal their identity. This is especially a problem with medical information of any kind as HIPSA (Health Information Privacy and Security Act) rules are very strict, as well as with credit card or bank account information.

I advise my clients all the time to only store the minimum data they need. Let other, bigger organizations store "risky" information. For example, take a membership site with a monthly recurring fee. If you take the credit card and store it "on file" somewhere and that credit card gets stolen somehow, then you could be liable for damages. However, if you allow PayPal to store the credit card and you only store the PayPal transaction id, then you can verify that their account payments are going through and if their credit card has a problem, it is PayPal's challenge to prove they didn't allow the credit card information to leak into the wrong hands.

Finally, never ever, ever, ever, ever, store passwords in plain text. This includes sending passwords between a login page and the authentication function in plain text. Even if you are using HTTPS, encrypt passwords before sending them over the Internet or a mobile data network. I remember reading a devastating story about gas station pumps when they first started taking debit cards. Specifically, some of them were sending the pin code from the pump to the building in plain text. Well some ingenious hackers figured out how to tap into that signal and stole hundreds of debit card numbers and pins before they were caught and the problem corrected. It is so easy now-a-days to encrypt passwords that no programmer worth their weight in pennies should be sending important data unencrypted. Period. End of discussion.

So what does this all mean for you? Well, if your software needs to store data of any kind, then carefully review it before, during and after development and ensure it is only the minimum necessary to get the job done. No more and no less. Any time information is sensitive or personal, think twice before storing it.

****

Remember
When in doubt, leave it out.

****

Power 2: Specify

So, do you have your clarity on your one to three biggest challenges? If not, please go back to the previous chapter and complete the observation and analysis steps. They are critical to saving you from spending unnecessary time and money building the wrong software. Nothing breaks my heart more than software that doesn't help, makes problems worse or *gasp* doesn't get used at all.

--- User Stories ---

The first step in any good specification is telling the story of the software from the users' perspective. At this point no thought should be given to technology, language, delivery platform (unless relevant to the story) or any other aspects of implementation. The more these read like short stories, the better the resulting software will be.

* *

Patience Pays Off
This step takes finesse and practice. In my experience, too many developers, and even experienced software companies, skip or scrimp at this point. No one suffers more than the end users.

* *

The purpose of a user story is twofold. One, it gives clarity to the design team: flow, most used features (which then need to be easily accessed and utilized), screen layout, size of buttons and text, and how images are incorporated, if at all. Two, it allows for "sanity checks" at key times in the design and development process. User stories are the best tool I have found to virtually guarantee software will be useful, usable and, therefore, used. This is one of the keys that will keep the team focused and produce the ROI (return on investment) you desire.

So how does a user story come together? Start with the problem, mindset or other motivation that gets the user heading toward the software. Then describe each step, each selection, and each decision along the way until the problem is solved.

--- Case Study ---

Relatively recently I was meeting with a life coach who helps people heal emotional traumas in their lives. She was intrigued about building a mobile application for her clients or prospective clients to connect with her between (or before) their healing sessions. We talked for well over an hour about possible features, but nothing resonated with her. Then it hit me. We just needed to step back and put ourselves in the shoes of the users. Really look at their perspective and their mindset when they would pick up their cell phone looking for her to solve some problem they were having.

Viola! Within minutes we were talking about her clients and how it wasn't unusual for them to be sitting up late at night thinking and spinning in circles and driving themselves into an emotional "bad place." So what is an obvious thing to do when one needs guidance for unsolved or confusing issues? Go to a psychic, of course. Get a tarot card reading.

Ok, so it might not be everyone's first choice, but what about harnessing this "mystic power" to get people thinking in other directions. To taking small actions to improve their situation and break out of the downward spiral. Bam! Perfect! She had already written weekly coaching tips the previous year. So now we had a pool of 52 tips and simple actions to pull from to create this tarot card experience focused around two to five minutes of healing activities a user could take while in emotional upheaval.

So here's how the user story reads... (Any resemblance to real persons is purely coincidental, and somewhat intentional. This is intended to be representational, not identify any specific individual.)

Sitting at the office. After hours. Stuck again trying to prepare a critical presentation for tomorrow. Dollars on the line. Possibly even my job. But I'm going nowhere! I'm going to end up working all night! I have got to break out of this funk so I can get some sleep or this presentation will be horrible even if the slides are right... What to do, what to do...

Oh! The healing card app. Sarah, my coach, said it would help.

- *Grab cell phone*
- *Click icon*

Ah, there's Sarah's photo, I feel better already. Hmm. One card for daily guidance or three cards for emergencies? This is definitely an emergency.

- *Select 3 card option*
- *Focus on my current situation and emotions... (Wait, click next?)*

- *Select first card (see image? and title?)*
- *Select second card (see image? and title?)*
- *Select third card (see image? and title?)*

Ok, here are the details.

- *See Title, Image, Wisdom, Action Step for each*
- *Take action step while reading through, for example a breathing exercise, physical movement, writing activity or other helpful activity to do for 30 seconds to two minutes.*

Next – Option A:

Wow, I feel much better. I am focused again and I feel like I can do this and it will be okay. Whew! Oh! I can let Sarah know how well this worked. What a great idea!

- *Click to send message.*

Next – Option B:

That's better, but I really need to work on this more. It just keeps happening over and over. Oh look, I can ask Sarah for more help.

- *Call now (if early enough)*
- *Or request a call tomorrow*
    - *Enter contact info*
      (pre-populated from data on phone, if possible)
    - *Select time of day*
    - *Send request*

Next – Option C:

Wow, that helped. I better get back to work!

- *Exit card app.*

--- K.I.S.S. ---

Only solve what needs to be solved. Only specify what needs to be specified. This is why the first step of preparing is critical. Sometimes the solution is simpler than appears on the surface.

A friend of mine runs a meditation and energy healing group on the east coast of Florida. She has about 40 people in her group who come off and on to her monthly meditation and training events she holds four to six times per year, mostly women, mostly over 50. She wanted to grow her group and to do that she felt she would need software to track her people and manage communications with them. So she started asking around for suggestions on CRMs (customer relationship management). *Salesforce, Infusionsoft, Batchbook,* and others were on the tip of everyone's tongues. Fortunately, I ran into her before she committed to monthly payments, extensive setup and a bunch of heartache when the results she longed for weren't there.

Instead, I asked her one simple question: **How do your current participants prefer to be contacted?**

Her simple answer: They rave about my monthly email newsletter and the one-page fliers I mail to them with all the details on the training events.

So then the solution for her CRM was also simple: *Constant Contact.* It is based on sending email blasts to groups of users who manage their own email addresses. New users can sign up from her website.

People can cancel whenever they want and she doesn't have to lift a finger (managing the email group in Outlook was one of her complaints). In addition, she was able to capture physical addresses for each person as well and then export from Constant Contact to Excel to do a mail merge for the mailing labels whenever she sent fliers for her event.

Simple problem (when the user story was told the right way) with a simple solution. The epitome of K.I.S.S. – *Keep It Simple, Stupid*.

--- Flow Charts, High Level---

Now it is time to step from pure English to pseudo technical. Specifically taking a high-level approach to flow charts. These should capture only the high-level elements. If a technical person, especially a coder, is involved at this point, then the tendency will be to get too detailed.

My favorite approach to these flow charts are post-it notes on a white board. Jot down one to three words to represent a step in the first user story. Stick it on the white board. Capture the next step, and so on. When the first user story is done, move to the second. The order really isn't relevant at this point. If you notice two steps are similar, but a little different, then split your post-it notes to capture the sameness and differences. In this way you can connect the flows and naturally, organically lead to the points of overlap.

Important note: You may find as you work that three or four of the user stories are pretty similar and one is quite different with little overlap. Feel free to put this outlier aside for now unless you strongly feel it is critical to the business. If that is the case, I recommend you look carefully at the other user stories and decide if maybe those are less important and you could focus on solving the outlier first.

Once you are satisfied that your flow chart represents the user stories, then bring out your list of problems and do a sanity check. Are the steps in this flow chart going to solve the key problems you identified? Hopefully the answer is yes. If not, you will want to go back to the user stories and capture the ones you missed and, of course, update the flow chart, before you continue.

****

Try It Out
Walk your team through the flow chart, especially a few people who were not involved in creating it. The insights you get from their questions can lead you to simplify and refine your results.

****

The complexity of the flow chart will be in direct proportion to the cost of the solution. Simplify here as much as possible—just be sure you are still solving the problem.

The final step of creating flow charts is to capture them digitally. In some cases, a photograph of the white board will be sufficient. In other cases you may want to use a program to recreate the wireframe.

****

Interested in Flow Charting Tools?
My current favorites can be found at
www.StickyLearningBook.com/resources

****

HINT: Don't get caught up in the "proper" symbols. As long as you are self-consistent in your use of symbols within your wireframes, that is all that matters. I have adopted my own standards for symbols. Feel free to use these or adopt your own.

Diagram 5: Simple Flow Chart Symbols

Starting Point

Online Step
Example: Enter name, email, etc.

Offline Step
Example: Phone call

3rd Party Service
Example: Google Maps API

Data Access
Example: Load list of users

Decision Point
Example: Is username already used?

Process Flow
Include decision result like "yes"
or "no" when applicable

Sometimes, I will use color to represent different user types. For example, "regular" users could have white elements, approval by a manager might be in a yellow box and an administrator unlocking a disabled account may be a black box with white text.

My only warning on the use of color is to do a test print in black and white to make sure you are not causing stress or confusion for anyone who needs to refer to the wireframes who may be fully or partially colorblind. The biggest no-no is using green to represent good and red to represent bad without any other indications of the same. If you want to do this, I recommend a dark green and a vibrant red so they print distinctly different in greyscale.

--- Case Study, Revisited ---

Here is an example of a flow chart from the case study above. As a reminder, this was for a business person feeling stuck and looking for some quick actions presented in a fun, playful way, to get themselves going in the right direction again.

Diagram 6: Flow Chart for User Story

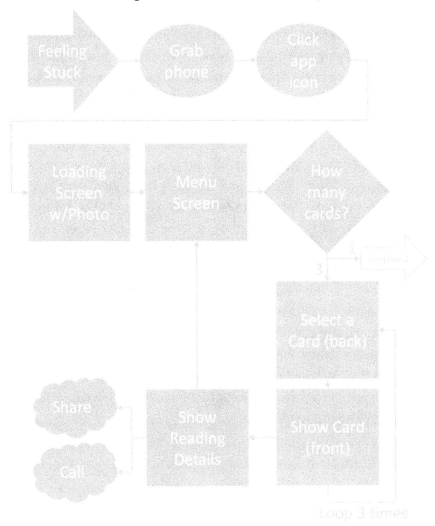

--- Choose the Best Technology ---

Most people at this point will have jumped into the final step already. That is a big mistake. Before you go about the "fun part" of creating the screens, you need to consider how your application (or applications) will be delivered to the users.

For example, you may look at your flow charts and realize that there are clear distinctions between the needs of the sales people and the needs of the managers. In fact, this is often the case. So to simplify the project, you can divide your application from one large application, trying to solve the needs of every user, into two or three smaller applications targeted to different types of users.

Especially important at this phase is to consider the funder of the application. For example, one of my projects was very well received by the project team and the end users. It even went through two rounds of upgrades over the years to add enhanced features. Unfortunately, all that stopped on a dime one day when the CEO tried to open the application on his iPad and it wouldn't launch. The project team—including me—developed this for the best technology at the time it was first conceived—specifically, Macromedia's Flex Builder (later acquired by Adobe and renamed Flash Builder). We got complacent and didn't upgrade to the mobile technologies as they were emerging. While we all made the best choices at the time, it is clear in hindsight that someone should have been designated to watch for new technologies so we could support them before all the funding got cut.

There are three primary sets of questions to answer before determining the best technologies:

Which device or devices will each type of user be using most often? Are there other devices that may possiblely be used? What is the estimated distribution?

Does this application need to run when disconnected from the Internet? If so, how soon will the user get connected again? Consider cases where a user might be out-of-network while traveling or otherwise out of the office.

Will a given device be used almost exclusively by one user? Or will different users be sharing the same device with different accounts? Will the user or users expect to return to the last thing they were doing, even if they exited the application or shut down the device between sessions?

Then you can decided on the technical details based on the above.

> ➤ Remember what the user did (session state) or not
> ➤ Many quick transactions or fewer longer ones
> ➤ Share current view with another user; what specifically
> ➤ Database type (MySQL, MSSQL, Oracle)
> ➤ Server language (PHP, Node.js, .NET, Java, RubyOnRails)
> ➤ And much more

--- Wireframes ---

The final step in the specification process is to produce wireframes. Just in case you are new to this term, think of these as blue prints, but less rigid. The wireframes should include each element you need on each screen, in each pop-up, each message, possibly reports or printouts, or any other parts of the software that a user will interact with.

The goal of the wireframes is to get to the most simple, understandable and USEABLE interface for your application.

The secret to making the best wireframes is NOT getting caught up in the exact layout. Put in the pieces you need. Don't worry if they are in exactly the right places, or the right sizes, or all the graphics are there. In fact, I often use a box with the word "logo" in it, instead of using the actual logo!

The uglier the better, for the wireframes. That way you can focus on meaningful discussions over what should and should not be on each screen without arguing over colors, readability or other factors that will probably be changed anyways when the real graphic designs are created.

There are a number of applications for creating wireframes. As of this writing, my personal favorite is *Balsamiq*. It has a wide variety of pre-made components, runs offline (so I can work any time and place I feel creative) and even has a free trial (which lets you be certain it will work for you before you invest as you will probably want multiple licenses for your team to collaborate).

****

Interested in Balsamiq?
Find out more at
www.StickyLearningBook.com/resources

****

Finally, include notes and arrows in your wireframes to capture important features or behaviors not readily apparent with just the layout. For example, "Update the search results as the user is typing," "refresh map as the user's position changed to keep their current position in the center" or "use 3D animation to show card flipping over."

--- Case Study, Again ---

Here is an example of one of the wireframes I created for a coaching card mobile app.

Diagram 7: Example Wireframe

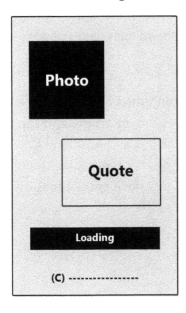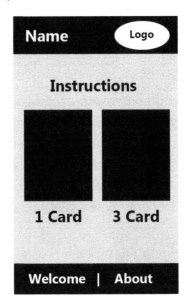

--- Features List ---

There is one final step I traditionally include in the specification phase. This is where a checklist is created. This checklist serves several purposes in future phases.

1) Estimating development time and cost
2) Laying out milestones and/or checkpoints for the development phase
3) Identifying APIs needed to access application-specific and/or third-party data
4) Making the best possible decisions for IT and programming languages to use within the application
5) Staying on track during development; reducing or avoiding scope creep
6) Verifying the completion of the work

The analogy for this is like an outline of a book. At the highest level, there are sections within the book. Then there are chapters within each section. Finally, there are subheadings—subsections—within each chapter.

My favorite approach—to ensure I don't miss any features—is to go through each image in the wireframes one at a time and capture all the features. Then I review the flow charts and fill in any gaps. Once I am comfortable that the list is complete, I reorganize the features list by feature type. Sometimes projects have special feature types, but most commonly I use types such as

- data / database
- content (a.k.a. images / text)
- API / server calls
- User Interface (UI) components
  Sometimes I even split these into "standard" and "custom", especially for more complex projects
- UI layouts (header, footer, sidebar, each type of screen, pop-up windows, etc.)
- reports / printouts
- loading / response messages
- error handling

One of the most overlooked aspects is the last in the list—error handling. Chances are you won't think of every possible error. If you have extensive experience in software development, you might get pretty close. So this is one area I expect to expand throughout the remainder of the project.

I do not consider good error handling to be scope creep. Instead, I estimate the project expecting that we've only thought of 1/2 the possible errors. Usually we do much better, but this allows for more difficult or subtle errors to be overlooked without blowing the budget.

--- Case Study, Final Look ---

With the completion of the features list, we have all the specifications needed for the coaching application.

I. Content
    A. Images
        1. Coach Logo
        2. Coach Headshot
        3. 36 unique card fronts
        4. Back of card image (one)
        5. Development company logo (for about)
    B. Text
        1. Short motto/saying on launch screen
        2. 36 card write-ups
            - title
            - 1 sentence about
            - 3-5 sentences of meanings/interpretations
            - 1 action
        3. About coach
            - bio
            - email
            - website url
        4. About development company
        5. Credit to individuals who built the application
        6. Copyright

C. Buttons / Icons
    1. 1-card
    2. 3-card
    3. Share
    4. About
    5. Facebook
    6. Twitter
    7. Email
    8. Call
    9. Another reading
D. Messages for Share and Contact
    1. Facebook message
    2. Twitter message
    3. Email message to share
    4. Email message for contact
II. API or Application Programming Interface
(i.e. how the application connects to data or other applications)
    A. Configuration file with card text and image filenames
    B. Configuration file for ads / specials offered by the coach
    C. Share
        1. Facebook
        2. Twitter
        3. Email
    D. Contact
        1. Email
        2. Phone
    E. Links
        1. Email
        2. Website
        3. Facebook page

III. UI components

    A. Icon Buttons

    B. Text-only Buttons

    C. Links

    D. Cards

    E. Text block (for card write-up)

    F. Label (for card title)

    G. Scrolling area for reading results

    H. Share Menu

    I. Contact Menu

    J. Progress Bar (for wait during launch)

IV. UI Layout

    A. Preloader (a.k.a Splash screen)

    B. Select Reading (includes about button)

    C. About

    D. Select card

    E. Preview card

    F. Reading Results (including share and contact)

V. Animation(s)

    A. Preloader/Splash to Main Screen

    B. Flipping card from back to front

VI. Error handling

    A. Ads fail to load: Hide ad area

    B. No network connection when share or contact clicked: Show "Please connect to the network and try again."

VII. Releases

    A. Builds

        1. Free with ads

        2. $.99 with no ads

    B. Stores

        1. Google Play Store

        2. Apple App Store

CAROLYN R. BORTON

Power 3: Evaluate

Congratulations! You made it through the most mentally taxing of all the steps in software development. Pat yourself on the back. Take yourself out for your favorite meal. Get ready to get back to the fun.

--- Sanity Check ---

Take a step back. Breathe. If possible, put this project on a shelf for a week. Then review the plan again from a fresh perspective. Don't look at it. Try not to think about it. When you review the materials again you will likely receive some fresh insights. Specifically in the form of critical features which are missing or not-so-critical features you can push into a future phase.

Also, use this time to revisit your cost of doing nothing. Realize that the design phase you just completed represents 20-40% of the entire application development cycle. So, ask yourself would it be worth completing this project if I had to spend four times again what I just spent on the design phase not only in money, but in manpower, resources and upheaval in your processes. If the answer is no, stop now.

If the answer is "I'm not sure," then pause longer. Revisit your specification documents and see what you can take out. If your remove half the items, then you can cut a quarter to a third (probably not a full half) of the remaining effort and budget to complete the project. Please don't get fooled into thinking you can cut half the remaining effort with half the scope. Software development is a lot like cooking a turkey. You cannot simply double the heat and half the cooking time. You'll end up with crispy outsides and a raw center—a totally inedible meal in the form of unusable software.

--- What Should You Look For ---

First, you look for existing software that is similar to what you want. As with information, no software is totally new. There will be someone else with similar ideas somewhere in the world. Now, they probably won't have everything you need and definitely won't have everything you want. But there's a 50% chance that you will find something that is worth trying for three to six months to see if the solution is "good enough." Especially if you are looking at a hosted solution that you only need to commit three to six months to. I recommend steering away from long-term contracts at this point. The best of the best software companies believe in their product so much so that they won't require two-year contacts (unlike the cell phone providers)!

Second, you look for experts in the industry. If you need custom software for your bank, then seek out the movers and shakers in the banking software industry. If they don't do custom development themselves, they probably know several people that do. Make sure you get their honest opinion and a story or two—don't settle for only a business card. Well, you can settle for it, but realize what level of recommendation (or not) that gives you.

Third, seek out software companies.

****

Looking for Outsourcing Recommendations?
For my recommendations, go to
www.StickyLearningBook.com/resources

****

Finally, once you have selected five or so software companies that are leaders in the right industries for you, then start talking to them about your project. Pass them your specifications. Answer their questions. Then watch for those who want to change the specifications. Ask for explanations why. If they can explain their reasons so that you are able to understand—and believe they are right—then put them at the top of your list.

After all is said and done, you should have at least three estimates for your project. Because of project changes at this point, these estimate probably will not be exactly the same as each other or your specifications. They will certainly not have the same cost, technology or milestones. Don't worry, we will sort this out in the decision step.

--- How Do You Know For Certain---

Nothing in this life is guaranteed. Least of all software development. We're talking about a crap load of 1's and 0's floating around at hyper speed, being smashed together and rearranged in an effort to produce meaningful and predictable results for completely illogical and unpredictable humans. Digging deep into the quantum mechanics behind computers, it has been postulated that it's a wonder that computers work at all. According to the mathematics, they shouldn't. Yet obviously they do as I'm writing this book on my computer and there's a really good chance a computer was directly involved in you reading it.

So then you ask, "Should I buy pre-built or create a custom solution?" "How do I know if I should be talking to solo developers or development companies?" "How can I be certain I am hiring the right person/company?" "What should I do if you don't like any of the options presented thus far?"

These are great questions. They should be asked. However, the answers are as much art as science. In other words, one should follow their gut feelings (art) as much as analysis and rankings (science). The experience to have a "trained gut" takes 7-10 years to accumulate. Perhaps if most of the time you are overseeing five or more concurrent projects of various sizes (taking anywhere from two weeks to two years) and teams (individual to more than 10, onshore, offshore and hybrid), then maybe you could get there in five years.

Until then my best advice to you is to do the analysis thoroughly and completely and then hire the trained gut of an expert who has no personal gain from the result of your decision. In other words, don't trust the sales guys—even if they are the technical experts—representing the people/companies you are considering. Instead, seek out an independent, third-party analyst. They do exist because I am one.

****

Get Help
Check out my recommendations at
www.StickyLearningBook.com/resources

****

--- Warning Signs ---

Finally, I highly recommend that you watch out for key warning signs and if you see any, please stop and investigate further. I could recount numerous stories of how brushing off even one of these as "my imagination" later lead to heartache, disappointment and even, in some case, the complete meltdown of the project before it was completed or—the worst in my opinion—building software that never got in front of its intended users.

Here is my top 10 checklist.

- ☐ Prices are difficult to find on the website (which is particularly important if you are looking at pre-existing software or software-as-a-service)
- ☐ Short answers like "yes we do that" or "of course that's included" to questions about features or experience when not followed immediately up by "here's how" or "let me show you"
- ☐ Negotiating cost with one person and specifications with another (on either team)
- ☐ "Let me look at this and get back to you," especially if it is in the first 15 minutes of a conversation
- ☐ Second-level tech support won't get on the phone until AFTER you commit to be a customer

- ☐ No clear exit strategy in the case of dissatisfaction
- ☐ Ignoring expert advice; Customers driving deep technical decisions: coding language, server, placement of buttons, etc. (unless the customer truly is an expert in that area and they stick to the area(s) where they have the expertise)
- ☐ Percentage ownership deals in exchange for cutting the development costs (only mediocre developers will do this and the customers will force the developers to do significantly more work than advertised)
- ☐ Customers who ask a developer to cut their costs for a custom software project because they could potentially resell it later
- ☐ Developers who won't show you their code

This is by no means an exhaustive list, so please add or edit it through your own experiences.

****

More Warning Signs?
If you'd like to tell me how one of these is useless or that I overlooked an important warning sign, please go to
www.StickyLearningBook.com/contact

****

Power 4: Decide

Making a decision may at first seem like a daunting task. However with the formulas I will share with you, it can become an easy task. It takes a bit of time, but the difficult parts are done... or rather they are if you follow a wise process for the decision making.

In fact, there is one secret that if you know it and embrace it, you will have a smooth experience and end up with software that you truly love. It may even become something you and your team cannot live without. If you ignore it, you may feel like you are in a horror movie, running through the woods after making the classic mistake to split up.

For in fact, this is what I am referring to. If you split up now and make the decision on your own, without full buy-in, you will be wasting your time, money and hard-earned sanity. But first, you need to prepare a smooth ride.

--- Prepare to Gather the Troops ---

Most business owners I talk to at this point think we need an "all hands" meeting right away. Let's introduce the candidates, get people's opinions. All I can say is "Hold the reigns, Tiger." If you want to kill the project with indecision, let's do it. In fact we're better off shaking hands and walking away now. The result is always the same: spinning cyclone of indecision, the destroyer of projects.

Instead, I have a tried and true formula for getting meaningful feedback (resulting in team buy-in) in a controlled and concise way. I learned this technique through parenting. In part from books, and then refined with experience.

Kids love choices, but give them too much freedom in the choice and you wait (seemingly forever) for a decision. Yet, given a simplified choice the whole family can be happy.

The same is true with teams at work. After all, most of us are still big kids at heart!

--- The Secret Ingredients ---

1. Binary decision, or at most 3 options
2. Clear upside(s) to each option
3. Clear downside(s) to each option

Here is a simple example of a decision that I commonly offer to my son...

Scenario: The time is currently 8:00 PM and bedtime is 9:00 PM.

Option 1: TAKE ACTION NOW. Pause the TV now, brush teeth, get pajamas on and otherwise get ready for bed. Execute with focus and you'll likely be able to finish the 8:00 to 9:00 programming using fast forwarding through commercials.

Option 2: TAKE ACTION LATER. Keep the TV on now and it will go off at 8:30 PM (not paused). Then get ready for bed and when ready go straight to bed. If there's any spare time, you may read in bed until 9:00 PM.

Clear upside on the first is TV until bedtime, with the downside of getting off the couch immediately and the risk of not finishing the show(s). Clear upside on option 2 is for sure finishing the 8:00 to 8:30 show with the downside of not seeing the 8:30 PM show at all (or recording it for the next day).

Interestingly, my son doesn't always make the same choice.

We'll get into the details of the choice to offer your team in a moment. Before that is possible, we need to finish the analysis and prepare the options.

--- Features List ---

All right, finally our hard work back in the specification step is about to pay off. We're ready to create ranked priorities lists where we have our must-haves, nice-to-haves, and other features.

Also remember to include the show-stopper features. These are those things that you will not accept in a solution, so matter how great the rest of the solution is. For example, when looking for a CRM (Customer Relationship Management) tool, my husband absolutely did not want per-user pricing. This made searching for solutions quite easy because we could seek out the pricing first and eliminate an option quickly, before wasting time digging into the details of the system.

The secret is to make a grid that looks something like the following:

Diagram 8: Feature Analysis Grid

Points	SHOW-STOPPERS
	MUST-HAVES (up to 50 points each)
	NICE-TO-HAVES (up to 10 points each)
	OTHER FEATURES (up to 1 point each)
	UNREQUESTED FEATURES (10 to -10, depending on level of benefit or harm)
	Total

The unrequested features will come from proposals, not your specifications, so simply leave 10-20 lines available for writing these down.

--- Maximum Score and Cut-off Score ---

Total up all the elements from your specifications to figure out the maximum possible score.

Multiply the maximum possible score by 0.8 to get the cut off score. Place this cut off score in the spreadsheet.

Also include a blank for the total score for the proposed solutions/companies which will be analyzed using this form.

I like to put the scores along the top along with the project name and proposed solution.

Diagram 9: Header for Feature Analysis Grid

Project Name: Worksheet Score:

Vender Name: Cutoff Score:

--- Gather and Analyze the Data ---

Make a copy of this spreadsheet for each potential vendor (who hasn't already been eliminated for one of the show-stopper or the aforementioned warning signs). Then go through the product information or the details on their proposed solutions and note which features they do and do not have.

Then tabulate. Give a full score to each line item whenever the solution fully meets the requirement. Partial score (usually half) if it can only meet the requirement part-way.

****

Hint for Better Tabulation
If you are finding many partial scores, then revisit the specification and see if you can split the requirements into several sub-requirements. You may find in this way that the elements fall into different categories, helping you get a better, cleaner scoring algorithm.

****

Next, go through each sheet and calculate a score. Compare this score to the cut-off score. If it is below, put this proposal aside and spend no more time considering or discussing it. Take all above-cut-off proposals into the next step.

TIPS

> ➢ Wait to calculate maximum score and cut off score until AFTER ranking all the proposals (this helps avoid bias during tabulation)
> ➢ Present proposals anonymously to the person or people doing the rankings (especially if they met any of the potential vendors during the evaluation phase)
> ➢ Have several people perform the ranking (each person must rank all proposals) and discuss results to come to consensus on each proposal's score

--- What if... ---

Ideally you will have two or three qualifying proposals at this point.

What if you have only one?

That's simple. This part of the decision is made and you can skip to the last element in this step. Unless of course you feel the need for debate. Then you can prolong the time and expense by seeking out another qualified candidate.

What if you have more than three?

You'll need to narrow down the list before continuing. Remember that two-way or three-way decisions are the best. You have two possible options, and you may decide to use both of them.

A) Adjust the grid to move a few items from nice-to-haves to must-haves and recalculate. Only re-calculate those that have NOT been eliminated, this is not a time to revisit the "trash."

B) Introduce other factors into the grid, such as location of the vendors (local, other part of the country, partially off-shore or fully off-shore), or communication and responsiveness. You may even consider "feeling" factors, such as how nice they were to your team or their apparent level of concern for the lowest paid employees who will use the software. Keep in mind that these may not reflect the development phase, especially with larger companies, as you may have been talking primarily to sales and marketing people up to this point.

As the grid changes, you will of course need to recalculate the maximum and cutoff scores as well as the scores for each proposal that is still in the running. Repeat as needed, but hopefully you are able to narrow down the pool in one or two iterations. Otherwise I will begin to worry about the success of your project because additional decisions will need to be made during the development phase.

If you find yourself spinning here, take a step back and consider again why you are doing this project now, its benefit and what would happen if you never finished it. If after all that you are sure it is right to move on, then continue and you should find you have new focus and clarity that speeds everything up.

Once you have two to three qualifying proposals in hand, stop second-guessing yourself. Just move on.

--- Now Engage the Team ---

Now we're ready to get the team involved in the final stretch. This does not mean a group decision. Rather, the focus is information gathering for informed decision making and a feeling of contribution from those who will be affected by the decision.

The process is simple...present the team with the "ingredients" of each option or candidate.

Ingredient 1: No more than one page per option.

Ingredient 2: No names of companies.

I like to use colors or shapes to distinguish the options as these do not imply a pre-conceived order of which is good, better and best. We find ourselves discussing the relative merits of the "Red Triangle" versus the "Blue Square" which is fun, in addition to being anonymous.

Ingredient 3: Overview of each candidate or proposal including benefits, downsides, risks.

Do not get caught up in individual features. Look back to the benefits these features accomplish (which you should have identified in the preparation and specification phases). You will notice that some benefits, and possibly even some downsides, will show up under more than one of the options.

Then retire the grids. Lock them up and ignore them. The exact scores of the qualifiers are no longer relevant.

Now gather the troops in whatever your normal culture dictates. This could be a team meeting, email blast, corporate retreat. It doesn't matter the format, what matters is that you clearly state the feedback you are looking for and hold everyone (even up through highest management) to this standard. If you are having discussions, politely let people know when they are going off-track and starting to rant about the misery caused by the current solution or drag the group off-topic.

****

Hint: Moderate with Character
I have found nominating a moderator who has a special object of some kind to hold up when someone is going off-track is a great way to notify people without having to interrupt them. This is your opportunity to add humor to the meeting by using a stuffed animal, a silly hat, a decorated "magic wand" or whatever your imagination can dream up.

****

The specific feedback you are looking for is:

> ➤ Across the two to three options in front of them, select the top five downsides and rank them in order based on how much pain they will cause you. Be strict about no more than five. Anyone with more than five will need to cut their list down to five. Less than five is okay, as long as the others are non-issues for them. This should be reported and gathered for further analysis.
> ➤ Discuss each person's number one downside. How it will make their job difficult or impossible and why? Dig for specifics. This can be a group discussion or individual reflection.
> ➤ Across the two or three options, what two benefits really excite them and will have a positive impact on their job, and why. Again, narrow it down to just the top two. Gather this for further analysis.
> ➤ To end the meeting on a positive note, allow individuals to share their top one benefit. Not everyone should be required to share, but you will likely find that everyone will, even if it's to agree with someone else's choice.

--- Final Analysis and Decision ---

Now take the top five downsides and top two upsides from each person. Look at how they fit to the vendors. In almost every case there will be a clear winner at this point. Personally, I put heavier weight into the negatives and look for the vendor with the least of these. However, this may be a cultural and personal choice at this point.

Once you have your decision, announce it and now you can share the software or vendor's name with your team. And the real fun begins...

CAROLYN R. BORTON

Power 5: Create

The creation of software is best achieved with clearly-visioned, well-defined, quickly-achievable sprints. **Clearly-visioned** means the goal is understood by every member of the team from the top "idea person" to the bottom "code monkey." **Well-defined** means that there is a checklist of for measuring successful completion. In some circles, this is called a test plan. **Quickly-achievable** means one to two weeks of effort, maybe a month.

****

Consider This...
How would you cover an elephant
with paper from head to toe?

Answer
One sticky note at a time.

****

Yes, there is a long-term goal of building an exceptional software product. And the first four steps of the process have laid out what will be required to make that happen. Now that the "rubber meets the road," so to speak, the only path to repeatable, reliable success lies in tackling one "sticky note" at a time.

Imagine you are in Washington D.C. Let's say, for instance, at the Lincoln Memorial. You're sitting on the steps, looking over the pond, enjoying the reflection of the Washington Memorial tower. And you think to yourself, I'd like to go to Los Angeles and stroll down Hollywood Boulevard.

Let's even say that you pull out your phone and map out the route. So you know where you're going and how you're going to get there.

Would you get in your car and start driving expecting to make it straight through without stopping? No, that's insanity right. First of all your car will run out of gas long before you've made it out of Virginia (or maybe a little further if you have a hybrid). Second, you certainly can't safely drive for three or more days without sleep!

And yet, most software projects are approached exactly this way. The leaders create a road map, also known as specifications, and put together a team, also known as developers. Then start driving as fast as they can. No stops, no breaks, no side trips to experience interesting sites along the way.

Please, don't feel badly if you are part of one of these trips already. It's not too late to wake up and change your experience. In fact, over my decade and a half of professional work in software development I too have been in involved in many projects that start or become the software equivalent of *National Lampoon's Vacation*.

--- The Bleeding Edge ---

One project in particular jumps out to me as a great example. The names have been changed to protect the not-so-innocent.

It was the mid-00's and 3D animated feature films were starting to take off. 3D immersive environments were wide-spread in console games. There was a buzz about the future of 3D delivered over the Internet.

It was around this time that I joined *eLance*. Through this site, a small group in Atlanta found me and hired my team to build a small prototype of a 3D "house": four plain, square rooms with the ability to look around and warp from room to room. It worked and we all became excited about the possibilities of this medium.

So the discussions began about what it would take to make realistic-feeling 3D environments and walking capabilities. It was a little beyond the edge, but not too far. Right?

As time went on and the project grew from one apartment to a virtual city... And the graphics had to be more and more realistic every day... And the responsiveness had to rival video games... It started to become apparent that our grand plans might not see the light of day.

The client refused to release without all aspects being perfect (as defined in his mind). Instead of focusing on one project, we jumped around from element a to b to c to d, back to a, over to c, and so on. Based on who was going to be at the table in the next meeting.

Fortunately, a few projects were able to be released, but I don't believe they ever received the publicity which was originally anticipated. Unfortunately about three times as many ideas were left on the table or buried in closets and left to shrivel.

Software that is new and innovative—ahead of its time—has a higher risk of failure because the technical components may not exist (yet) for it to be fully successful. It could be challenges with hardware; it could be limitations in network speeds. It could be (as in the case of the 3D projects) that the consumers were a bit uncertain and unwilling to commit. No one wanted to be the first to dive in and play full out. It turned out they all wanted someone else to be that leader, so they could follow. Because of the risks on this edge, projects may "get cut" before they reach their full potential (as ours did). This led to the term "the bleeding edge".

The good news for you is that you need not experience these trials yourself. Whether or not you take on a project on the bleeding edge, the solution is the same. And it crosses any software medium. I have figured out the solution, and it has worked every time I've used it.

--- Single Item Focus ---

Focus with full and complete effort on one component, interface element, logic flow, or functional element of the project at a time. Completely build and thoroughly test this element within a one to two and a half week time span (never more than a month). This block of time and effort can be called a sprint.

How do you choose what to start with? List your features in order, and start at the top. Tip: When one sprint is complete, re-evaluate the features list and select the next element to receive full and undivided attention. So the original plan you set can and will change over time. This is another key to the success of this approach because you are always able to work on the one most important thing.

You may end up with a somewhat different solution than the original plan. This is a good thing because it will undoubtedly solve the underlying problems, challenges or frustrations better.

Is it easy to predict the budget? Well, that depends on your perspective. Each sprint is clearly defined and therefore easy to predict. And because you make the choice to continue, evaluate, receive user input or anything else between each sprint, you are in totally control of the budget at all times.

My recommendation is to allocate a long-term budget during the preparation and specification periods. This overall budget would be reflective of what makes sense to spend to solve the problems, instead of leaving them alone and doing nothing.

What I almost always find with this approach is that upper management is happy the whole project because they will see about 80% of the results after 50% of the effort. Then when the next 80% (of the remaining 20%) is achieved in the next 50% of the budget they will be pleased to allocate additional budget to continue refining the solution and solve more problems as well.

By the way, this is called the 80% rule of software development.

****

The 80% Rule of Software Development
For every half of the budget you spend, you can get
80% of the way from where you are to the completion
of the project, a.k.a. bug-free software.

****

Let's review the numbers...

> First half of the budget = 80% complete
> Second half of the budget = 96% complete

> ➢ Third half of the budget = 99.2% complete
> ➢ Fourth half of the budget = 99.84% complete

If we examine a small- to medium-sized project with 10,000 lines of code, the 99.84% complete means 0.16% incomplete which equates to 16 bugs. However, the astute observer may notice that four halves is the same as 2 times the original budget. If we stopped back at the end of the original budget, the software was 4% incomplete. That may not sound like much; however, it is equivalent to 400 bugs in 10,000 lines of code.

--- Now What? ---

If you are like me when I first heard the 80% rule, it really depressed me. I thought, "How do I ever release a quality product which is 4% bugs (96% complete)?" And, "No one will ever pay twice what they originally planned just to get rid of the inevitable bugs that creep in. How can I run a profitable business when everyone will want me to do half the work for free?" Maybe you are thinking, "I have to allocate double the budget! Where will those funds ever come from?"

Fortunately I did not have to wait long to find the answers. Specifically it comes back to the power of sprints.

1. Allocate a reasonable overall budget.
2. Use a part of it for each sprint.
3. Adjust the sprints as you go to focus on the one more important feature at that time

This mitigates the risk. Worse case, doubling a two-week budget only takes it to a four-week budget; doubling a one-week budget only takes it up to two-weeks. And this would be with a clear and conscious decision because of the pause after the first one to two weeks to evaluate the next priority. Sometimes that next priority is continue with the current feature set and make it more stable. Most of the time it will be to move on to the next feature.

Another advantage of sprints is that the features will become available to users over time (after a certain minimum number of sprints). Therefore you will start to see ROI (Return On Investment) before the project is even completed. This means that by the time you are nearing the end of the original budget, there will "magically" be more budget available because the ROI is at work and compounding with each day.

--- Tracking and Communication ---

It may be no surprise to you by this point that I have a rule for communication. Keeping projects on track is challenging and this rule is designed to allow course corrections during the sprints. And during the planning and specification phases as well, come to think of it.

****

8/3 Rule for Communication
Connect with the client after every 8 hours of work
or 3 days of calendar time, whichever comes first.

****

This means that during a development sprint, the client and project lead are talking every day. Sometimes twice a day, in fact, depending on the size of the team working on the project. Between sprints, especially when waiting for feedback from real users of the software, the interested parties are connecting every 3 days, which is the same as twice a week. This keeps the project top-of-mind and the process flowing smoothly. When too much time passes without discussing, there can be a feeling of "where were we" and precious time and effort (and budget) is lost to coming up to speed again.

--- Tools of the Trade ---

One of the first questions that comes up when software engineers gather is "what tools do you use?" As a field we are always seeking the next best thing, because someone we know probably built the next best thing. In this light, I have decided to keep my thoughts about the specific tools on the website, instead of in print where they quickly go out of date.

That being said, there are certain types of tools that are a must-have for any successful software development project.

> **Version Control** – This is where copies of all the source and release files are maintained. This is important for disaster recovery. If a computer dies, only a small amount of work is lost. If the software becomes unstable, the developers can go back to a previously stable version and re-introduce changes and fix instabilities along the way. This saves countless hours of headache. (That's my experience talking!)

> **Ticketing System** – This allows feature requests, bugs and ideas to be captured and organized. A well, utilized system will also provide information for reports on the status of a project and whether it is heading toward or away from stability (based on the 3-way ratio of verified-complete, ready-for-testing, and active/in-progress tickets).

- ➢ **Development, Staging and Production Servers** – These are 3 separate places for code to be deployed for testing and use in the real world. The Development Server is where different layers of code come together. I can be working one minute and down the next, but the developers are on top of it the whole time. The Staging Server is updated as stable version of the software are available (after testing on development server). Before the first release, this is the end of the line. After the software is put in front of real users, there will also be the Production Server. This is very stable and changed only with new releases of the software.
- ➢ **Time Tracking** – This is how budgets are managed.
- ➢ **Document Repository** – This is where the latest specifications are stored. In some cases it may be an additional folder in the same system as the version control.

****

My Favorite Tools
For a list of the tools I use, go to
www.StickyLearningBook.com/resources

****

--- Proper Architecture ---

Finally, no book on software would be complete without a discussion of best practices.

I have lived, breathed, and dreamt software engineering for almost two decades. My life—and my gift—are software architecture and creation. Perhaps you remember the story from the Introduction about how I fell asleep during the midterm and still set the curve for the class?

Here are the principles I insist are followed in every software project I lead:

- ➢ **Object-Oriented** – Functionality is broken into chunks to be managed more easily. At the highest level are packages such as UI (user interface) and DF (data façade). Within UI there are sub-packages such as screens (or views), windows, and components. Within DF there are sub-packages such as loaders, models, controllers, dtos (data transform objects), and vos ("virtual objects" transferred from server app to client app and vice versa).
- ➢ **Abstraction** – One part of the system is not required to know the inner workings of any other part of the system (e.g. login doesn't care how user lists are loaded and displayed or vice versa).
- ➢ **Encapsulation** – Each object has one primary purpose and to other objects only need to know how to communicate with it. The "how it works" is not necessary to understand (unless you are the programmer writing that object).
- ➢ **Single Source Data** – Any specific piece of data is stored in only one place in the application. (e.g. username is only stored in the User model). In some languages this means singletons and whenever possible this is achieved through binding.
- ➢ **Error Handling** – To ensure errors are caught and handled, plan for errors before coding starts and test for them first as the code is being written.
- ➢ **MVC-L (Model-View-Controller-Loader)** – This is a variation of the MVC design pattern which abstracts the loaders into separate classes and allows the backend that is used to be

"swapped out" to another language or service without affecting any of the rest of the data or user interface.

➢ **Test Harness** – This goes hand-in-hand with MVC-L. Specifically it is a version of the backend system which loads static files. In some cases this serves as all or part of the unit testing (including automated unit testing).

In every case where we've used a Test Harness we were glad we did. In some cases we didn't, we paid a hefty price. The biggest benefit comes when the server side is under control of a different set of developers. Because we are able to point to our known-working data with the change of one configuration variable, we can a) prove a bug is on the server side or b) quickly debug client-side bugs by introducing a new file into the test harness and running the application locally (minimal network delays).

Some of the principles in my list are common in the world of software development. Others are in part or entirely my own. Either way, I believe in them deeply because my team and I have successfully built and released numerous (over 100, I believe) different software projects using them.

There are many more design patterns and principles out there in the world. There are even whole languages created to enforce certain behaviors in the programmers. These are a topic for another book on another day.

****

My Musings on Software Architecture
To read, listen or learn more about my
principles of software architecture and design,
visit www.StickyLearningBook.com/resources

****

--- In Conclusion ---

This brings us to the end of our journey through the creation step.

You may notice that "Release" was not one of the elements we've discussed. This is because I believe that the software development cycles never ends.

A "release" is a brief moment in time. While it should be acknowledged and celebrated (parties are awesome!), it is not the end-all-be-all goal of software development.

Instead, I invite you to focus on constant and never-ending improvement. This means going back through the cycle to come out better each and every time:

- ➤ To adapt and change with the advances in hardware.
- ➤ To embrace new thoughts and new approaches to solving our challenges in business, learning and life.
- ➤ To listen to the learners and grow to better meet their needs

--- Until Next Time ---

I hope you have enjoyed this journey with me as much as I've enjoyed writing it for you. My wish is that you will take the steps and processes I've shared and grow them and make them your own. I know I will be doing the same.

****

Stay in Touch
Please feel free to reach out to me with your questions, comments or stories any time at www.StickyLearningBook.com/contact

****

CAROLYN R. BORTON

About The Author

Carolyn R. Borton is a successful entrepreneur with a passion for educational software. Her company, Sunshine Learning Systems, specializes in creating engaging educational applications for private schools and small businesses.

Carolyn got her start in educational software in 2000 as a lead software architect for PLATO Learning to pioneer their expansion into web-delivered immersive learning. She also created interactive science modules for Pearson, and partnered with schools and school districts to produce customized learning programs. Carolyn designed and built applications for the United States Department of Education, World Bank, USAID, World Wildlife Fund, Land O' Lakes Foods, St. Jude Medical, and a variety of small businesses.

Carolyn currently resides in Land O' Lakes, Florida where she enjoys the company of her loving husband, Jason, energetic son, Benjamin, and their two dogs, Franklin and Penny. Her hobbies include reading science fiction and fantasy novels, and studying Krav Maga with Ben (see photo). She likes to relax on cruise vacations.

Carolyn's favorite success principle is Constant and Never-Ending Improvement. Her personal mission is

Exceptional Software, Revolutionizing Education

www.ingramcontent.com/pod-product-compliance
Lightning Source LLC
Chambersburg PA
CBHW071203050326
40689CB00011B/2227